PLAY BETTER SCRABBLE®

by Michael Goldman

British National Winner 1977
British National Runner-Up 1979
British National Highest-Game Scorer 1981

Reproduced, printed and bound in Great Britain by Cox & Wyman Ltd., Reading

Published by Michael Goldman, 32 Maple Street, London W1.

Graphics by Martin B. Sandhill Art and Design Services Telephone 01-455 1601

ISBN No 0 950 89740 X

Contents

Chapter 1

So you know how to play Scrabble®! Well, now let's proceed to examine those techniques which will improve your game to the level of a master or grandmaster. Firstly, you must abandon what is probably your usual aim – trying to trample your opponent into the ground – because this aggressive style leads to a mental block which channels your thoughts away from an open constructive method of play.

You must think of yourself as an architect designing groups of letters intended to interlock in the most fruitful way. These groups of letters will not usually be precast on your rack of letters but must be arranged on the board to make the most openings for a letter to be played before and/or after them. For example, suppose you have the letters RYAW; you could make WARY but you could also make AWRY, so you should play WRY, retaining the A for placement on the next move; TRAP becomes RAPT so you play RAP, keeping the T to place after or before it; GRAINED is also READING, which accepts the letters A or B or D or T before it and an S after it; MANGIER can become REAMING, thus allowing a C or a D to be placed before it, or MEARING, taking an S before it.

It doesn't matter that these openings will also be available to your opponent – experience will show you that often he or she will block some, or use them unfruitfully, or even not see that some letters will specially fit some openings.

You must make as many openings as possible on the board, because you will need them for the seven- or eight-letter words that you must try to create in order to score more highly. It is obviously more sensible to have two or three openings than to have only one which may quickly be rendered unusable by your opponent.

Some people will comment, "That's not Scrabble®!" Well, it all depends what you understand Scrabble® to be. In my opinion it is a game of word-chess, but unlike chess it gives the players the power to develop possibilities of letters and words in ways that give more pleasure and excitement to the creator than the sole stimulus of beating an opponent. If winning is everything for you, as it is with some players I know, then this book is not for you – and yet, in a way, it *is* for you, because if you master my style, you will also win most of your games. The change won't happen overnight, and it won't be painless; it hurts, initially, to explore the various ways of using letters in a new fashion, as I know from experience. While you are learning you will find yourself losing lots of games and sometimes suffering ridicule from uninformed and unteachable exponents of the old-fashioned methods. But persevere – it will be worth it in the end!

Let us proceed to map out the procedures by which a new magic may enter your game. It is necessary to use both Chambers and the Shorter Oxford Dictionaries for fairness and comfort. This is something not yet practised in Scrabble® competitions because of lack of judges, time, etc., but here we are not so unduly circumscribed.

We will start with the most useful two-letter words. I am not trying to slight your intelligence by using two-letter words, because they are what I term open-ended words as opposed to dead-end words. Each one is capable of accepting a letter before or after it, so that each will have a double opening for a seven-letter word to be placed above or below, or to the left or right of it, whichever the case may be.

The following two-letter words just revel in the art of constructive Scrabble® and they also, except for YE, have the facility of being contained in innumerable nine-letter words:–

AN AT EA EE EL EN
ER IN NA RE WE YE

Let us take an AN and see what I mean. You can make an AN with two letters from the seven on your rack or you can create it by using an A or an N on the board and merely adding an N or an A respectively from your rack. You will thus retain either five or six letters on your rack. With these five or six letters you have varying chances of obtaining a seven-letter word with the replacement letters you get. Obviously it would be preferable to use only one letter from your rack to create AN if the remaining six letters have a reasonable chance of making a seven-letter word with the replacement letter you will receive. Should you have P X I T Y I N, it is no use executing the above ploy, but if you have R E T I N A A then by using an A to make AN on the board you are doing yourself an excellent favour!

Believe me, please, it is far cleverer to score only a few points and obtain one or two letters from the bag to juggle with those remaining on your rack, or even to use to create an opening for later, than to score perhaps 6-20 points by using four letters from your rack. You may disagree with this philosophy but have you considered the rapidity with which the good vowels and consonants frequently get used up? And think of the number of occasions on which you mutter, "If only I had an E!" Advanced players know only too well the foolishness of four- or five-letter words scoring only 7-20 points because they often see their opponents making them, and bemoan the futility of wasting such good letters. I am not suggesting that you confine your play to making two-letter words all over the board. No! Merely intersperse the two-letter words into your normal game. When in doubt, make a two-letter word!

Perhaps you knew that already, but maybe did not appreciate how much more valuable it is to score 2-10 points and create a dual opening than to score 15-20 points by using three or four letters. You may also question the validity of conducting this operation frequently instead of scoring more highly on occasions. Here you are absolutely correct, but you will discover that this problem rarely occurs as the letters on your rack and the state of the board will lead you, quite rightly, to play three-to five-letter words for higher scores. Let me make it perfectly clear that I am not advocating continual use of two-letter words whilst trying to make a seven-letter word on your rack. This is a style of play affected by some players who know no better and their games usually end by their making either very high or very low totals, most often the latter. I am emphasising the creative value of using only one or two letters at a time instead of wasting three to five letters, and then only when your remaining five or six letters have the makings of various seven-letter words if you pick up one or two popular letters.

To show you what I mean, let us return to the example given above; I said that if you have R E T I N A A on your rack you will be doing yourself an excellent favour if you use just the A (preferably to make an opening). A little thought wil lshow why – the letters B, C, D, E, F, G, H, I, J, K, L, M, N, O, P, R, S, T, U or W when added to R E T I N A will make ATEBRIN or RABINET, CERTAIN or CRINATE or CITREAN or NACRITE, TRAINED or DETRAIN, TRAINEE or RETINAE, FAINTER or FENITAR, TANGIER or GRANITE or INGRATE or TEARING, INEARTH, INERTIA, JANTIER, KERATIN, RATLINE or LATRINE or ENTRAIL or RETINAL or RELIANT, MINARET or RAIMENT, ENTRAIN, OTARINE, PERTAIN or PAINTER or REPAINT, TERRAIN or TRAINER, RETINAS or RESIANT or RETAINS or RESTAIN or STARNIE or RETSINA or STEARIN or NASTIER, NATTIER or NITRATE or TARTINE or TERTIAN, RUINATE or TAURINE or URINATE o URANITE, TAWNIER or TINWARE. Remember RETINA! With RETINA you have an eighty-five per cent chance of picking up a 'right' letter. Not bad!

I can find no other combination of six letters which operates as favourably as RETINA without using an S but the idea is operable with popular groupings of letters selected from the letters, A, E, D, G, I, L, N, O, R, S, T.

The obvious beauty of a grouping like R E T I N A is the likelihood of getting the three consonants and three vowels because of their preponderance among the hundred letters, forty-eight letters out of one hundred to be exact!

What has been said about two-letter words applies equally or more importantly to open-ended three-letter words. The following are the most important:-

ALE   AVE   EAR   IDE   LAM   LOT   LOW   OPE   REE

You will observe that some of them contain two-letter words from either or both dictionaries and it cannot be overstressed that a three-letter word accepting a letter at either end is a formidable friend on the board as even if your opponent uses one end you can often still use the other end.

You will not always be able to follow these principles. If you have letters like B I W Y I O Q on you rack, you should change all the letters and bide your time. Remember, your aim is to have on your rack effective letter-groupings; there are certain rules which can help you greatly. To avail yourself of the best chances of obtaining those letter-groupings, you should rid yourself of C, F, H, J, K, P, Q, U, V, W, X, Y and Z as soon as possible; J, Q, K, U, V, W, X, Y and Z should not be retained on your rack for longer than one move or you will be handicapping yourself for no good reason. Another useful rule is not to keep ING on your rack for more than two moves as it is often wasteful to do so. Subject to the conditions of the board you should always try to keep popular groupings of letters on your rack at all times and you will be surprised at the frequency of seven-letter words turning up. I am sure you will also be disgruntled by their not turning up but it is the percentage game you should be playing. Every player has his days or even weeks when little seems to go right and the moans and groans are familiar to all of us. Don't despair, the percentage will get you there!

Special attention should be paid to creating a three- or four-letter word leading to the triple-word avenue, as frequently you can gamble on your opponent not having one of the few letters that can be slotted before or after it, while you have one on your rack. Often the letter S on your rack may be the only letter which can be added to a noun (not some verbs which can also take D and sometimes R) and you can gamble that your opponent does not have one of the other one to three left in the pool of unused letters. A specific example of my point is the word LAIR, which will only take an F or G before it – if you have one it is worthwhile gambling. Develop your own collection of pet unusual words of four or five letters and you will find them a treasure-house as time goes by.

Here is a selection of my favourite two- to five-letter words (derived from Chambers) so that you can see exactly what I mean and which words take which letters before or after, or both.

(B)			(B)		
(E)			(D)		
(G)	EL	(D)	(F)		(L)
(S)		(K)	(M)	ANA	(N)
(T)		(S)	(P)		(S)
(Z)			(S)		
			(T)		
			(W)		

(G)			(D)		
(H)			(F)		
(K)			(H)		(N)
(N)	AE		(L)	OUR	(S)
(S)			(P)		
(T)			(S)		
(V)			(T)		
(W)			(Y)		

(B)	(ABY)		(L)	AKIN
(G)			(T)	

		(D)	(F)		(P)
		(L)	(M)	OU	(R)
(S)	AI	(N)	(S)		(T)
(T)		(R)	(Y)		
		(S)			
		(T)			

(A)	LOW	(E)

I must revert to the importance of six-letter groups on your rack as this is the so-called secret of getting seven- or eight-letter words. There are many players who will regularly get bonuses in most of their games but they could greatly increase the frequency of the bonuses by giving further thought to this formula. For further example let us take the six letters A S T E R N; how many players would use some or all of these letters to score with, but it is so simple to exchange the seventh letter (if it is A, F, J, Q, X, Y, Z) for any one of B, C, D, E, G, H, I, K, L, M, N, O, P, R, S, T, U, V or W to create, among others, BANTERS, RECANTS or

TRANCES or NECTARS or CANTERS, STANDER or STERNAD, EASTERN or EARNEST or NEAREST, ARGENTS or GARNETS or STRANGE, ANTHERS or THENARS, RETAINS or its various anagrams, RANKEST or STARKEN or TANKERS, ALTERNS or ANTLERS or RENTALS or STERNAL, MARTENS or SMARTEN, TANNERS, ATONERS or SENATOR or TREASON, PARENTS or PASTERN or TREPANS, ERRANTS or RANTERS, SARSNET or TRANSES, NATTERS or RATTENS, NATURES or SAUNTER or AUNTERS, SERVANT or TAVERNS or VERSANT, WANTERS. You have an eighty-four per cent chance of making a seven-letter word.

You may say that I am taking an unfair advantage by including an S in the six letters. I am, but how often does one use an S to score only 15-20 points? Far too often, because it is too rarely appreciated that an S in your possession means that you only have to make most verbs or a pluralisable six-letter word with your other six letters and you are there!

There are many other six-letter groups, both with and without an S, which give you a very high chance of developing a seven-letter word but these will be considered in Chapter 10.

Don't let your sights stop at seven-letter words. There will usually be letters available on the board which can be intermingled with your seven letters to make an eight-letter word. It is helpful to be familiar with the common endings of such words – here are the most useful:

ATE ANT ED ER ERS EST ENT IDE IED IER IES ION ISE IST ING ILY LET NCE RED SED TED

Remember the prefixes OUT UN IN EN OVER PRE PRO RE UNDER and that it is surprising how many words end with ABLE OR IBLE.

You should take each usable letter on the board, picture it on your rack and then continually re-assemble the eight letters to try to make a word. Initially you may find your brain is stiff and resistant to this style of address. Perservere and slowly you will find that it will be exercised into easy movement until the process becomes automatic and the only lubricant needed is practice during play.

While carrying out this procedure you will come across eight-letter words that you could make if only one of your letters were different. Stop! Think! If there are two or three letters that would make all the difference then would it not be worthwhile changing that awkward letter in the hope of acquiring a useful one? It may or may not. Each case depends on the number of letters left in the bag and on your opponent's rack compared with the number of letters that will serve your purpose. Work out the odds! If it is more than a three to one chance it is usually not worthwhile gambling unless you have a lot of leeway to make up in the scores. Don't worry that if you do exchange successfully for that lucky, lovely letter, your opponent's next move may stop you making your eight-letter word. More often than not your opponent has his or her own problems or will go somewhere completely different. Sometimes, of course, you will pick up that delicious letter only to find that your avenue is blocked. Well, you can always talk about what you missed!

Are you fretting that other people always seem to be able to make anagrams but you can't? Well, maybe you can't but you can improve your anagrammatical ability, bad as it may seem to you. Anagrams are similar to weight-lifting; anyone may strengthen and develop·their muscles by training. Granted there are natural weight-lifters who start with a marked avantage but our brains are roughly the same size while our bodies are very different. We will devote substantial time to anagrams later on, where the skinny physique will be shown how to develop into a well-proportioned muscular frame.

I have now outlined briefly the basic principles which I believe can help you to play better Scrabble. The remainder of the book will deal with all the principles in more detail, but first it may be as well to remember one point; we have been speaking as if the game takes place in unaltering conditions throughout its duration but of course it does not and different tactics are relevant to the different stages of the game. These tactics will be considered more fully later on but here are a few points for you to consider now.

Have you thought about the need to start the game with a word which can be added to at either end instead of one end only? Or that your opening word can be the cause of a cramped game? For example, the word WON is an anagram of NOW but which is the better word to start with? WON will only take an S or a T after it but NOW will accept an A or E or K or S before it and an L or N or T or Y after it, which can make a vast difference to the consequent ease of moves. Never start with a word like DUG!

Perhaps you are nodding your head but bemoaning your seeming talent for obtaining racks like I O I U A E I which makes nonsense of any attempt at starting structure. These may leniently be termed 'impossible' so accept them as such and don't continue to fret over them. In such a case retain the A E and change the other five letters. If you obtain similar vowels then don't repine. Change again! It is far better to miss two moves in succession than to gloom and gloom while aggravating the badness of your rack and torturing yourself with increasing despondency. From the later chapters and illustrations you will observe what to do with any rack of letters.

The middle part of a game is very important, especially with regard to the 'big four', J, Q, X and Z. These four handicap your chances if you retain them on your rack during this period as they are nuisances despite their high points values. They should be used up or exchanged as quickly as possible as they reduce your chances of getting bonuses and restrict you from dipping into the bag containing those lovely S's and blanks. The middle-game only too quickly leads to the end-game which has a character all of its own and should be studied with more care than usual since it is here that a winning position is often lost and a losing position transformed into a winning one. These parts or periods of a game will be analysed later on so that you may come to understand their special nature.

Now we will have an illustration of good play to ease you gently into the saddle.

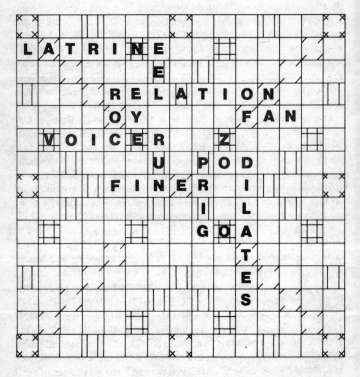

Figure 1

I draw the letters F I N E A T E and as it is my first move I could score 14 points with F I N E or 12 points with F I N, leaving myself nicely with E A T E so that an E could go after F I N with whatever word I make next. But my opponent is likely to have a D, E or O to place after F I N or to place a two- or three-letter word above or below it so I will try my luck by placing F I N E and hoping my opponent will position a four- to seven-letter word at the end of F I N E so as to give me a good chance of creating a seven- or eight-letter word with whatever I pick up to go with my A T E.

My opponent, with V R C P R I G, could make R I V E R (8 points) leaving himself with C P G, or F I N E R / P R I G (19 points) for example, or even retain R I G to go with the N and exchange the V R C P. Let us suppse, quite reasonably that he opts for F I N E R' / P R I G.

I pick up U I N L making E L A T I N U. Here the E L A T I N is very useful as with an A, B, C, D, E, F, G, O, P, R, S it will make A N T L I A E / L A N I A T E, B L E A T I N G, C L E A T I N G, D E L A T I N G, I N F L A T E D, E L A T I N E, I N F L A T E, E L A T I N G, E L A T I O N, P L E A T I N G, P A N T I L E, L A T R I N E, S A L I E N T, S T E A L I N G, among others. If I place the U after the G I will spoil the usefulness of the G in making an eight-letter word. I can place the U before the N thus opening the way for me to position my T or N over it. I do.

My opponent obtains O L E A to go with his V R C and utilises my U N by making V O I C E R and R U N. Never mind! If the U N had not been on the board he might have used the G.

I pick up Y, unluckily, and rather than make F A I N T L Y scoring 26 points, I prefer to play the Y over the E of V O I C E R, making Y E because it will take D, E, L, N, O, R or T over it at some stage, preferably soon by me! At the moment my score is only 22 compared with my opponent's 43 but that does not matter because I am trying to be constructive.

My opponent now has A Q ? I N O Z and can make Q U O I N, Q U I N A, Q U I Z, it is not worthwhile his using the blank for only 34 points so, sensibly he plays Z O / P O scoring 35 points and leaving himself, hopefully, with A Q ? I N.

I pick up an O, making E L A T I O N. I have five placements, E L A T I O N / O Y E for 72, E L A T I O N / E Y E for 72, E L A T I O N / T Y E for 73, E L A T I O N / A Y E for 72, or E L A T I O N / L Y E for 64 points. A moment's thought will show that E L A T I O N / E Y E is the best positioning, to allow an R or D or G to be later put before E L A T I O N whilst bringing E L A T I O N over to the right-hand side of the board. An S could go after it and not one S has yet appeared. Yes, I know I've stopped a D going over Z O but the Z remains usable.

My opponent now has A Q ? I F N and is in trouble! He decides to create O F / N A / F AN for 24 points, retaining Q ? I N. This is disputable as he might have exchanged the Q F N and reasonably hoped for three useful letters to intermingle with his retained A ? I N. However some letters can be placed after F A N, namely D, E, G, K.

His score is now 67 to my 94 and I have collected A I L D S E O. There are many small scores I can obtain in various parts of the board but I must play the O after the G making G O; A, B, D, E, G, O, T or Y can be placed after it. If I place the O over O F then C, G, H, L, P, R or W can go over O O F; but I have A, D, and O for G O and only L for O O F. My score is 99, but A I L D S E can receive various letters to allow a seven- or eight-letter word to be created.

My opponent has picked up R O M and it serves him right! Only too frequently does this happen when one retains a Q, even with a blank on one's rack. Now what can he do? He could exchange the Q M and he should but he has espied R E L A T I O N / R O C / O Y scoring 28 points and foolishly does this. His score is 95 to my 99 and he is content to have almost drawn level. As we know, such contentment is short-lived in Scrabble!®

I pick up an E and am disappointed but I make E L, knowing that B, E, G, S, T, Z can be placed over it.

My opponent has selected E R making Q ? I N M E R. Now he is obliged to exchange the Q M and he obtains L A – he has a variety of possible seven-letter words but he has to await my turn.

I get T and can make I D E A L I S T or I S O L A T E D or D E T A I L S. I go for the highest scoring combination of P O D / G O A / D I L A T E S, thus scoring 76 to give a total of 177.

My opponent finally settles for L A T R I N E / E E L, scoring 69 points. He could have made other words to go over E L but placing the E of L A T R I N E over E L and making E E L is the most open move, leaving, F, H, K, P, S to be placed over E E L. The scores are 164 to 177 and we will leave the game there, for it has served its initial purpose of demonstrating some of my principles in action, I hope!

2
The Start

The start, by which I mean not just the first move but the first few moves of each player, is much more important than most players realise and probably determines the nature of each game to a large extent. It must be appreciated that most games tend to gravitate towards the right without our really knowing why. Perhaps it is because we read from left to right and/or most players are right-handed, but it is a statistical fact that the left-hand side of the board, especially vertically, is least favoured by most of us.

This frequently leads to an odd pattern of interlocking words from the bottom left-hand corner to the top right-hand corner with entries and exits being blocked or difficult to utilise. To counter this tendency you should express a bias towards the top left quarter of the board from the inception of the game, if you can. Whatever words you start with should, subject to your other letters, be positioned as far left as possible, even if it means losing a few points in the opening scores.

How often have you said of a game that it was awkward or unrhythmic or unsatisfactory? Often it is because someone started with a three-letter word lik F I B or C A W and letters such as S or L or K were not quickly available to add on to these words. Instead, both players have to fiddle around trying to make two- or three-letter words with the vowels or consonants on the board and then find one side or more is blocked or rendered awkward.

It is better not to start with a three-letter word if it will not accept letters both before and after it. The simple word T A N should be looked at afresh at the start of a game as it also makes A N T which takes B, C, D, G, K, L, P, R. V or W before it, plus A, E, I or S after it, while your poor T A N only takes A, E, G, K or S after it. Suppose your letters are F I B C P T T – do not make F I B, B I T, T I C, P I T or F I T. Although O can go before T I C and E, S or K after it while P I T will receive S before it and A, H or Y after it, you will be left with unworkable letters on your rack: F B P T or F B C T.

When the game starts you have the best opportunity of exchanging letters for a varied selection and the most chance of getting favourable letters for those that you swop. With F I B C P T T you should retain I T and exchange F B C P T, and the odds of vastly improving your stock are heavily in your favour.

Similar reasoning applies to commencing with a four-letter word, although here there is a trifle more scope to expand. Even if you can begin with a four- or five-letter word to make the game reasonably open from the start, you should hesitate to do so if it means leaving a bad grouping of letters on your rack; e.g. F I B C P T O will give you T O P I C or O P T I C but it will leave F B on your rack. Yes, I know you can make F I B or F O B with the next move provided your opponent does not easily stop you by his particular play, but he usually will and you have F and B waiting to receive five letters. How many seven-letter words do you know that contain F and B? Not many! With F I B C P T O it is better to retain I T or I T O and exchange the others. I personally find the letter O not very attractive in formulating seven-letter words but here it is optional.

It is a good rule to think of R E T I N A A as being the best and easiest casting of letters to get at the beginning of a game because they constitute forty-eight out of the ninety-eight letters (excluding the two blanks). If you work your way towards this grouping so far as you reasonably can then for the first quarter of the game it is a good tactic. For the second quarter of the game it depends on how many of these forty-eight letters have appeared on the board.

Why am I so insistent on R E T I N A? Because the most desirable object of the game (apart from a triple-triple word) is to obtain the fifty-point bonus by using all seven letters on your rack. This is most easily done with R E T I N A as six of the seven unless you are lucky enough to have an S. If you do have an S or a blank you should still work towards obtaining the letters R E T I N A on your rack. Naturally you will try to get the vowels and the consonants together and not separately.

Should you be fortunate enough to start with an S or a blank or both on your rack then you should use neither in your first move. You are well along the route for a fifty-point bonus with an S or a blank to start with and if you have both then you are halfway there. If by using the S and other letters you can score more than 35 points then you may do so but not otherwise. If you can score 50 points or more by using the blank then this is also permissible.

Say you start with W P N S A T E. You can make a variety of words such as AWN, WEPT, PAWNS, SPAWN, SWEPT, SPAN, SPATE. If you place PAWNS on the board you will score 26 points, leaving yourself with T E, but you will have committed a cardinal sin. If you play PAW for 16 points, retaining S E N T, this is reasonable for you can place your N or S after PAW unless your opponent plays A, K, L, N or S after PAW or spoils it by some other move. Should you play W E P T, keeping S A N, then this is also reasonable as your opponent can only position one of the remaining three S's or the two blanks in front of W E P T. With either

P A W or W E P T you also have a good chance of making a seven-letter word with S E N T or S A N as the foundation, or an eight-letter word using such letters as your opponent leaves available after his move.

However, what if you retain N S A T E and exchange the W and the P? It would take too long to calculate all the possibilities but at the start of a game you have a very good chance of picking up two helpful letters to create a seven-letter word. Even if you only obtain one helpful letter, you will have six letters towards a seven-letter word. As luck may have it you could pick up two unfavourable letters, even another P or W, but such letters as you obtain may well be usable on the board, or you could even exchange again.

"Exchange again!" I hear some of you saying. Why not? At the start of each game lies your best chance of making the fifty-point bonus. Stop and think of all the games you have played which become blocked or semi-blocked halfway through, as well as the innumerable times when there was absolutely no chance of playing a seven-letter word on the board towards the end of the game.

Perhaps you are worrying about your opponent racing away with good scores while you are exchanging letters. I am not asking you to make a career out of it, merely to accept that exchanging twice or even three times (if your opponent is faltering) at the start is good play.

It is good play for a number of reasons.:

1. It is better than scoring a few points and retaining difficult letters.

2. A seven-letter word usually provides five, six or seven letters or ways that offer openings.

3. A seven-letter word usually scores 60-90 points.

4. Two moves instead of changes may both score badly and/or make the board unwieldy.

5. You are exercising your anagrammatic muscle.

Please don't descend into the obvious pitfall of exchanging repeatedly as a mania; two or three times is enough if you start first, while twice should suffice if your opponent makes the first move. Have you noticed how fluent a game is on the rare occasions when you both start with a seven-letter word? It is because the board is so wonderfully open and usable at will.

Sometimes it is of merit not to score as highly as might be possible, while opening the game as much as you can at the start. If your opponent starts with a three- or four-letter word then you should try to open it vertically or horizontally as far as possible, rather than play two or three letters on top of or beneath it to score highly. One cannot overstress the value of stretching out the words to make the highest number of letters further usable.

For example, if your opponent starts with A N T you could place L E A above it, thus

LEA

ANT

– but this should not be done. Instead

L

A N T E

A should be played for a few points less, as B or P may be positioned above L E A and D, F, K, L, M, N, P or T below it. The A and N of A N T E are still usable for inclusion in eight-letter words or would permit a seven-letter word to end above or beneath the A or the A and N. The few points lost by this gambit will be amply rewarded by the later moves freely allowable by the better opening structure.

Should your opponent position a five-letter word to start with, then it is also wise to open it up or down or sideways even if you score ten or fifteen points less than you could otherwise have done. You will more than make up the scoring differences on subsequent moves. Anything which tends to cramp the words or usable letters also tends to cramp your scores and leads to a peculiar pattern on the board which does not blossom towards the triple-word squares.

An open board will also help the Q, Z, X and J to be played more easily and quickly and enable them to be used again and again for their point values.

Mentioning the Q, Z, X and J reminds me to advise getting rid of them at the start for low scores or exchanging them as quickly as possible. They are not wanted at the beginning! Nor also are B, C, F, H, K, L, M, P, U, V, W or Y. Why do I include L and M? Because, oddly enough, they do not assist much in the composition of seven-letter words at any time, but especially not at the start.

How can one absorb the importance at the start of A, D, E, G, I, N, O, R, S, T and the two blanks? Perhaps by looking at them now and thinking how easy it is to make seven-letter words from them. I wish I could take any seven letters from the ten vowels and consonants and say that I could always make a word. Not quite – but very nearly. The first seven letters consitute A G O N I E D. I can't make an anagram out of that, though perhaps you can. The next seven, after excluding the A, comprise D E G I N O R, which is E R O D I N G. Then comes E G I N O R S, which is I G N O R E S or R E G I O N S while G I N O R S T makes S O R T I N G or S T O R I N G. Obviously one can carry on by taking any seven out of the ten letters in many ways, and making many anagrams very easily. Try it for a little while and you will convince yourself of the facility of these letters. Should you take any six letters and add a blank, you greatly increase the chances of seven-letter words.

From this we may also draw the corollary that these ten letters are worthwhile components at any stage of the game.

3

The Middle Game

Let us try to define this period as that which comes after the first three and before the last six moves of the game.

This period may alternatively be referred to as the 'counting' period as, subject to the letters on your rack, you will often be thinking of a specific letter which would make you a seven-letter word if only you were lucky enough to obtain it. This type of thought is folly. For every one occasion on which you are fortunate enough to get such a letter there will be ten occasions or more when you will be disappointed.

There are one hundred letters in the bag and the distribution of letters is shown on your board or in the rule-book. At any stage of the game it is simple arithmetic to calculate your chances of obtaining the one, two, three or more letters required to create a seven-letter word on your rack. By one, two or three letters I mean being able to make a seven-letter word by picking up an A or an E or an S, for example, not trying to get an A and an E or an A and an S. You should never try to get two particular letters together to make a seven-letter word.

In fact, it is a rare occasion when you should try for one letter to form a seven-letter word with the six letters remaining on your rack. Players do this too frequently and are often rewarded with two to four consecutive moves that are low-scoring, while they never get the appropriate letter they require.

By counting the letters already on the board and your rack you may soon see your chances of getting the letter or any one of the letters you need to make a seven-letter word. Usually the odds against you doing this are more than two to one and should not be accepted. If you have a two to one chance then take it but only take it once unless your opponent has coincidental troubles, when you can afford the luxury of a double try. The same reasoning applies to eight-letter word formation.

In effect you should not be trying for one or more particular letters to make a seven-letter word, you should be trying to form groups of letters which can contribute towards creating a seven-letter word, should they receive reasonably fitting letters to accompany them. There will be times when you cannot do this; for example, if you have F E Z I N T X you have to use FEZ, FIZ, NEXT, ZEIN, FIX, NIX or any other combination which scores highly without being too conscious of the letters remaining on your rack.

Should you have the Q in this period then get rid of it! Even if you don't score many points, it is far better to use it for a low score, or exchange it should you not have a U, than to keep it. Hope may be eternal but the game is limited and the Q is a nasty customer. If you can use the Q so as to leave it available for re-use then do so, although you may sacrifice a few points in specific placement.

Obtaining the J or Z or X during this period can be awkward, for they do not fit easily into enough seven-letter words to make their retention worthwhile. They should not be retained on your rack unless you can make an opening which will avail you much should your opponent not use it. At maximum you should retain any one of them for only one move.

The letters B, C, F, H, K, L, M, P, U, V, W and Y are 'blockers' on your rack and should be removed at the first opportunity by use or exchange. Never retain any of them in the hope of making a specific high-scoring word!

During this middle period you will be forging the nature of the end-game and you should also be constructing openings capable of taking seven-letter words. This period is often abused by players cramping or blocking the board without thought of later play.

If you look at the examples at the end of the chapter you will see only too clearly what I mean by opening the board and making the best use of your letters. So many players make a seven-letter word during the end-game and peer vainly for a place to put it. They may mutter their disappointments without realising that they are reaping the fruits of their earlier bad play.

Don't be frightened of exchanging letters! Your opponent will not race away from you to become uncatchable and may well be experiencing snags equal to or even worse than yours. A game in which players have not had two or more exchanges each is either a badly played game or one of those rhythmic games where words seem to flow like free wine – usually the former. The nature of the distribution of the hundred letters makes it essential to exchange letters from time to time without feeling fear or shame.

There are four S's and two blanks in the bag and by the law of averages (which frequently does not exist in Scrabble®) you should get your share. Your entitlement to such share diminishes naturally as the letters are used up but it is during this middle period that most of them emerge. They will emerge by chance as you use up letters or exchange letters so why not try for them while they are available? Frequently they don't appear on the board during the first few moves so they are still lying in the bag waiting for you! Far better to exchange now, with hope, than during the end of the game when most or all of them have been used up.

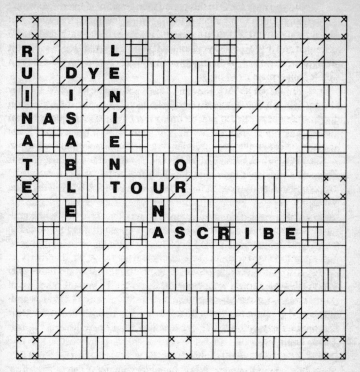

Figure 2

We will now look at some examples of play during the first third to half of the game:

Player 1 starts with O U R L I D S so he plays O U R, knowing that he can, if he gets the chance, position his L, D, or S befor O U R in his next move. He has got rid of the difficult U and retains L I D S which is a reasonable collection provided he obtains an A or E or O among the three letters to be picked up.

Player 2 is lucky! He has L E ? I E N T and has the option of placing it after O U R so as to make O U R N, which will accept B, M, Y before it, or creating L O U R or T O U R which will respectively take C, F and A, S before them and E, S, E and S after them. He then decides to make L E N I E N T / T O U R so as to open the board to its maximum and hopes to use an A before T O U R (A T O U R is in the Shorter Oxford).

1 has collected B A N to go with L I D S and although he can score 13 points with B A I L S / T O U R S, leaving himself with N D, or 19 points with B L I N D S / T O U R S, he merely places the N under the U making U N, available for his A or S to be placed after it. He may also be able to position his B or D over U N but he would obviously need an E or an O to go before the R of T O U R.

2 picks up R A I E O Y S and can score 32 points with S O I L Y, leaving himself with A R E, which is not to be sneezed at, but he places his Y before the first E of L E N I E N T, thus retaining R A I E O S. He can place any of his letters except I before Y E, or his A or S after U N or befor T O U R, or the S after T O U R if he is lucky enough to pick up a letter making a word with R A I E O S. Also he realises that he could perhaps make an eight-letter word with the letters L, N. I or E of L E N I E N T.

1 has got an E to go with B A L I D S, creating D I S A B L E. he cannot have B A L D I E S for though B A L D Y may be an acceptable pejorative it is not yet an accepted noun except in Websters Third New International Dictionary. Now, should he place it before Y E, making D I S A B L E / S Y E for 84 points or D Y E / D I S A B L E for 92 points or under U N or at the end of T O U R for much lesser scores? True, D I S A B L E and U N A only score 67 points but leave the way clear for another word containing an S or D to create D I S A B L E S or D I S A B L E D, and the other word could go along the double-word score line. D I S A B L E / T O U R S also only scores 67 points but leaves the triple-word score easily available at the bottom. It can also receive an S or D after it and permit access to the double-word score line. Player 1 plumps for 92 points with D Y E / D I S A B L E and contents himself with the fact that the E of D I S A B L E could be used in an eight-letter word starting with many letters, as well as the possibility of D I S A B L E being added to. He does not think much of the L of D I S A B L E receiving two letters before it to reach the triple-word score and nor would you. He dimly perceives that the E of D I S A B L E will permit a seven-letter word starting with A, B, E, H, M, N, O, R T, W or Y and that the L E of D I S A B L E may take a seven-letter word starting with ES, EN or ER preferably.

Player 2 has now, unfortunately, selected a B to go with R A E I O S and cannot make a seven-letter word with his B R A I E O S no matter how hard he tries. Maybe you can? He can make B R A I S E / T O U R S or B R A I S E / U N A for 15 points but he could also pick up a C, D, H, L, R, S, T or Z instead of his O and then would have ASCRIBE, BRAISED, BEADISH, BAILERS, BRASIER, BRASSIE, LIBRATES or BRAIZES with other eight-letter word possibilities. If he places the O before the R of T O U R then he can utilise this by placing his B over it to make B O R. He does so.

Player 1 has obtained A A I R N E T. He remembers R E T I N A as being able to accept, B, C, D, E, F, G, H, I, J, K, L, M, N, O, P, R, S, T, U or W to make a seven-letter word. By actually counting the letters played and the A on his rack he finds that he has fifty-one out of seventy-three chances of picking up a usable letter. But what to do with the A? It could be positioned before the S of D I S A B L E, which would enable him to use the triple-word score unless his opponent used it first. He thinks his opponent is going for a seven-letter word because of the placement of the O over the R of T O U R, but he reckons he has a better chance with R E T I N A than any other grouping of six letters his opponent may have. Even if his opponent uses the triple-word score he can always utilise O R or U N. He decides to risk it!

Player 2, luckily, has obtained a C which makes A S C R I B E. He can make A S C R I B E / O E for 68 points leaving the top triple open for a nine-timer or he can make A S C R I B E / U N A for 66 points and plumps for the latter.

Player 1 has got a U to go with his ´R E T I N A and can make RUINATE, TAURINE, URANITE or URINATE. If he plays RUINATE an E may be placed between the E and the L of D I S A B L E allowing a seven-letter word, starting with an E, with B or H or N or R or T or W or Y as the second letter going before the E of D I S A B L E, to descend over the left-hand corner double-word square. He therefore plays R U I N A T E, we will leave the game here in this wide open state.

* * * *

You start with D I K O I C E! It can happen! All to often we get a bad collection of letters at the start. It is foolish to struggle with a grouping like this for to place K I D and retain O I O E or to play O K E and keep D I O I is making trouble for yourself. Here, it is best to retain only E D and exchange K O E O I. We obtain E D J Z A S S, which is not wonderful but we must await our opponent's turn to see if he is faring better.

He has V A N O F T D and it is essential here to get rid of the V and the F in order to retain a reasonable grouping. He can't! Not by using them in a word to be placed on the board. So it is sensible to exchange some letters, especially as one's start in each game is more important than most people realise. Here, it is prudent to retain A N T and exchange V O F D, though a case could be made out for other exchanges. Our opponenent now has the letters A N T M I L E assembled on his rack.

From E D J Z A S S we play J A D E S for 42 points and keep Z, S.

Our opponent creates L A M I N A T E for A N T M I L E and the A on the board; you may see other possibilities but I can't. He has been lucky!

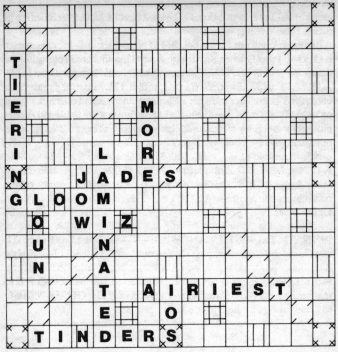

Figure 3

He thinks that as we have used a D and S in J A D E S it would be opportune to bring L A M I N A T E down as far as possible, so he does.

Z S has collected O E W E U. Well, that's Scrabble®! Out of various alternatives we play W I Z for 35 points, getting rid of the W and Z for a reasonable score and having to keep S O E E U.

Our opponent's seven fresh letters are S I N D T R R and here the best play is to place an R over the E of J A D E S so wit ill make R E and accept A, E, I O or U over it and D, P, S, T or W after it, although only an I or an O can go under the S of J A D E S.

Our S O E E U has acquired A L and although S O U L / S W I Z scores 22 points it leaves E E A on the rack and with derring-do we will keep S E A and exchange O E U L.

Our opponent's S I N D T R has obtained a blank so thankfully he creates T I N D E R S / L A M I N A T E D for 86 lovely points.

S E A receives O O I R and the gamble has come unstuck but we can make O O M / J O W, getting rid of the two inutile OOs and leaving the way clear for B, D or L to go before O O M while retaining the useful group of S E A I R.

The other rack receives L O U N I O N and the best move is to play L O O M / L O U N; it gets an insignificant 12 points but leaves space for the G to go before L O O M and our opponent can keep the useful I O N.

S E A I R gets O T and although O A R I E S T could be the superlative of O A R Y it would create great dissension and it is better to place the O over the S of T I N D E R S making O S, so at least the retained I can be placed above O S. Possible alternatives could have been O S / O T A R I E S or N O T A R I E S / Z O.

Our opponent's I O N meets with M E T G, so if he places M O above R E, making M O R E and keeps I N E T G, he will have a chance of making an eight-letter word with the available letters M, O, R or A on the board.

Our A R I E S T receives an I making A I R I E S T, which we gratefully place above the O S making A I R I E S T / I O S.

T E I N G acquires I R to make R E I T I N G. Twist it, turn it and he still can't find a word ending in I N G to fit onto L O O M except T I E R I N G. If he looks elsewhere he discovers that our A I R I E S T has provided him with an S to go after I G N I T E R or he can use the M of M O R E to making M E R I T I N G. However, T I E R I N G / G L O O M is best with 85 points.

We will leave the game here and look at another example.

* * * *

Player 1 starts with I S A E L U M. That seems very close to a seven-letter word but I can't find one. It is wasteful to play any word like M U L E, retaining I S A, or a five-letter word ending in S like M E A L S or M U L E S so as to score 20 points by using the double-letter square. How about the word L U M (in both dictionaries) which, among many other possibilities, will take the A or S before it or the S after it? Player 1 plays it, positioning the U under the double-letter square in case he has the misfortune to pick up the Q.

Player 2 has A R A I N E D and with a little thought will see that he must place an A over the M so that he is opening a choice of avenues for his next move – he will be able to put his A before L U M or his R or D or N over A M

Player 1 has drawn P L T and I S A E P L T is one A short of making P A L L I A T E S by using the L of L U M; P A L L I E S T as the superlative of P A L L Y would be generally frowned upon, as would P A L I E S T as

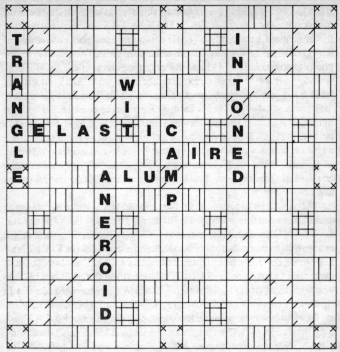

Figure 4

the superlative of P A L Y (meaning divided by vertical lines). It is frustrating not to make a seven-, eight- or nine-letter word out of such promising material, especially as the P or A or S can be placed before L U M or the P or S after it. Desperation! What to do? Eventually, Player 1 puts the P after A M making A M P, so as to be able to position his L or T over it while also being able to put the A or S before L U M or the S after it.

Player 2 with R A I N E D, obtains an O which develops into A N E R O I D and gratefully places this before L U M, so creating A N E R O I D / A L U M.

Player 1, with I S A E L T, receives a C and a little twirling makes L A C I E S T – surely that should be acceptable to his opponent? Maybe not and then who is to judge? Most dictionaries do not show comparatives and superlatives. He tries again for a seven- or eight-letter word and E L A S T I C springs to mind! Much safer' Just for fun he looks at A L U M and lo and behold the word C A L U M N I A T E S leaps into being – eleven letters! He could make E L A S T I C / C A M P or E L A S T I C / L A M P or E L A S T I C / T A M P, thus obtaining different patterns on the board for manoevering, or plump for C A L U M N I A T E S, just stopping short of the triple-word square. Most people could not resist making an eleven-letter word just for the joy of it but resist it he must. The letter G can be placed before E L A S T I C and the letter S before or after C A M P and, what is more, the G would come down the triple-word line. With a heavy heart but a sense of virtue he plays E L A S T I C / C A M P.

Player 2 draws A G I O I R I and little use can be made of this. He can make G R A I L for 12 points, R A D I I for 8 points, G R A T E for 12 points or many others. He toys with the idea of using R A D I I, leaving himself with G I O; this would open the bottom treble just in case his opponent had a G for G E L A S T I C. But there are only 3 G's and it is unlikely that he has one of the remaining two! He decides to keep G R A I and exchange O I I.

W I ? E I O T has appeared for Player 1 and there is little he can make with it. It is essential to get rid of I and O and preferably the W as well but this appears impossible. He could use W I to make W I T, which might enable him to insert the T over it in the next move to make T W I T, and hope that ? E I O T will obtain two fruitful letters. I O T could be placed to construct I O T A, allowing a D (in Chambers) to be slotted over it, but this would mean retaining the W, a clumsy letter. W I is placed to make W I T.

G R A I collects T E R making G R A T I E R for Player 2, and I can see no way that he can make an eight-letter word. If he keeps G R E A T and uses or exchanges I R he will have some good chances. By retaining T E A R I G he could only hope for an N or a blank to make I N G R A T E / G R A N I T E to fit onto E L A S T I C. The letters G A R R E T would require an E or S to create G R E A T E R or G A R R E T S or G A R T E R S. It seems to be a mental toss-up. However, he decides to utilise the I R by placing them after the A of C A M P, so making A I R, which can accept E, T or Y after it (the E only in the Shorter Oxford).

Player 1, with ? E I OT, fortunately stumbles on N D and has a variety of possibilities. Firstly, he might try to use the blank as a G, hoping to use the triple-word line. No luck! Then there is E N T O I L E D or I N T O N E D / A I R T or M O T I O N E D or I N T O N E D / T W I T or D E N T O I D S or R A T I O N E D, among others I can't see. A favourable opening-placement is I N T O N E D / A I R E to make the board more open without hampering its present possibilities.

Player 2, with G R E A T, has been blessed with ? L. G R E A T ? L will make T A N G L E R / G R E A T L Y / T R A N G L E and probably others I cannot see but T R A N G L E is a beauty! Placed to make T R A N G L E /

G E L A S T I C it is wonderfully vulnerable for an S to be placed above T R A N G L E on the triple-word square thus tripling S T R A N G L E in addition to whatever other score is made. At this promising point we will leave the game and move on to the next example.

* * * *

You start off with A E R A T E I; you could change an E or I or A and hope for better things but exchanging any one of these three letters will be very risky. Changing the I means you would be hoping for a C, D, L, S or X for A C E R A T E, A E R A T E D, L A E T A R E, A E R A T E S or E X A R A T E – seventeen chances out of the remaining ninety-three letters. Changing an E woould leave you with A R A T E I and and the hope of a D, N, S or V to create R A D I A T E (T I A R A E D), R A E T I A N, A S T E R I A or A T R E S I A, V A R I A T E – sixteen

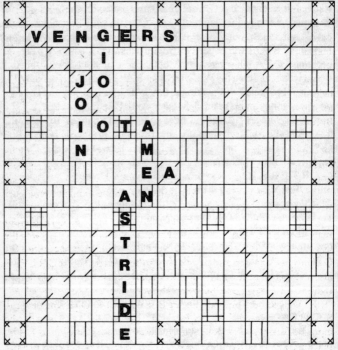

Figure 5

26

chances out of ninety-three. To swop an A for an E or N, making E T A E R I O, R E T I N A E or T R A I N E E is even worse with fourteen out of ninety-three chances. I may have missed some but not enough to make a vital difference. So it is best to keep A E R T I and exchange E A or, perhaps, place it as an opening word quite usefully and not needlessly allow your opponent to start with a double score.

Your opponent has R N O I D M N, which is not very useful. To make M O R N or M I N D or I R O N and place any one on the board is not fruitful, nor does it augur well for the future. Better to shed M N by making M E N and keep R N O I D; the M E N will accept A or O over it and D, E, G, T or U under it. Also it does not interfere with E A accepting letters after it, nor does it greatly handicap E A taking a consonant before it as vowels can go before the M and N.

Your A E R T I has been cursed with I O and a little thought doesn't seem to make it look any better. The best you can do is probably I O T A/ A M E N, only scoring 12 points and I O T A only permitting a D before it (Chambers only) and A M E N only accepting D, E, S or T after it. This would leave I R E on the rack. That is your best bet because otherwise you will have to go through the motions of trying to exchange I O to obtain two useful letters to go with A E R T I, which is not R E T I N A yet and may never become so.

Your opponent, with R N O I D has attracted J S which is not very helpful. He should not make J O I N T for 28 points with the T of I O T A, for it leaves him with R D S and despite the S that is still three consonants. By making J O I N with the O of I O T A for only 22 points he would retain R O D S but block the E A. If he creates J O I N by utilising the I of I O T A for 22 points he can keep R I D S, does not spoil E A, and J O I N will be able to take his S from the triple-word square if need be, or to accept a T from the same source.

Your I R E receives G O E S, making I R E G O E S and any four-letter word ending in S could be placed from the triple-word square to fit onto J O I N for a fair score of 25/31 points, but you spot the word G I O on your rack. If you place I O/J O for only 11 points you retain G R E E S with the G available to go over I O (B will go over I O as well). A strange point – G I O is only in Chambers and B I O is only in the Shorter Oxford. G R E E S is also a very good combination of letters (apart from being a word in its own right) to await two more. So you make your move.

R I D S has been blessed with A T E, making T I R A D E S or, perhaps, S T A I D E R, but definitely S T A I R E D or A S T R I D E and maybe more. So finally your opponent may take advantage of the lonely E A by placing T I R A D E S to make T I R A D E S/T E A/I N or merely placing A S T R I D E to make A S T R I D E/A N, putting an E two squares ahead of the triple-word square. Earlier we noted A M E N could accept D, E, S or T after it so that the R of T I R A D E S would be followed by D, E, S or T in an eight-letter word. It would seem more useful to have the R rather than the S in that situation but it would not bring the E of A S T R I D E onto the bottom line. The number of eight-letter words having E as the sixth letter is large and your opponent has as much chance as you have of using the E except that it is your next move. However, he reckons that since you place I O to make I O / J O you probably have a B or G to place above I O, so he may as well develop the bottom-line opening in case you use the I O opening.

G R E E S draws V N which doesn't look hopeful until you realise that you have V E N G E R S, or R E V E N G E S by using the E on the bottom line for 89 points. Yet V E N G E R S / G I O, though it scores 80 points, delights in accepting an A in front of V E N G E R S and the A would go down the triple-word line. Let us be creative and not play protectively or blockingly. V E N G E R S / G I O it is.

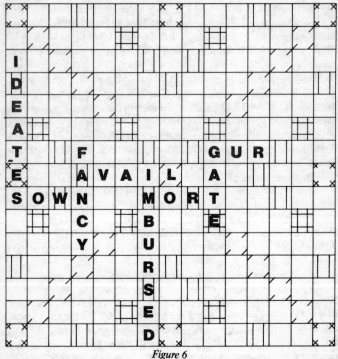

Figure 6

28

Player 1 begins with V I A L A N E which is not stimulating but should not be dispiriting. He has A N V I L, N A V E L, N A V A L and many more. He needs to get rid of the V and an A so as to leave himself with a useful letter grouping. Here he should not use a five-letter word such as A N V I L for 18 points as it is an impotent opening. He should forget V I A L but think of V A I L, which takes an A before it on the next move, or A V A L which likewise would take his N. As A V A L is an adjective (Chambers only) he opts for V A I L, which will receive an S at its end. So he plays V A I L, retaining A N E.

The other rack is also uninspiring – G O T T R E D. It is not worthwhile for Player 2 to make G O I T R E (D), G R O V E (D), V O T E (D) or suchlike, nor merely to place a T under the A on the board leaving him with G O T R E D, because a quick run through the alphabet will show that only an I to make G O I T R E D will enable him to score highly. G O T R E D is therefore a bad grouping but he remembers that O R T takes many letters before it, of which his remaining D and T are two. By placing O R T with the L making L O he paves the way for his D or T to be inserted after the I of V A I L to, perhaps, make an eight-letter word containing I D or I T.

A N E has drawn F C R Y making F A N C E R Y – a pity it does not exist. Here, there is nothing constructive that can be done, especially as F C Y are bad letters for using together or separately in eight-letter words. Unavoidably Player 1 must exchange or play F A N C Y / A V A I L for 23 points or I F / F O R T Y for 24 points. Either way he is using up an opening but F A N C Y / A V A I L gets rid of the C in addition to the shedding of F Y in I F / F O R T Y. I know that I F / F O R T Y leaves an A or O to go above the Y for a five-letter word to reach the triple but the C is a bad letter so it is best to get rid of it. He decides on F A N C Y / A V A I L.

Player 2, with G T E D, has drawn A E A, forming A G A T E D E. He could play A G E / A Y for 13 points, allowing his remaining D to be placeable after A G E or before A Y, or play A G E with the T of O R T to create G A T E, which only gives 7 points but permits his A to go above for A G A T E or his D to go below for G A T E D. The latter move seems slightly more open and favourable as his opponent could have a B, C, D, F, G, H, L, M, N, P, R, S or W to place before A Y.

Player 1's R E has received M B U ? S making BUMMERS, RUMBLES, IMBRUES, IMBURSE, ERBIUMS, CUMBERS, LUMBERS (SLUMBER), NUMBERS and UMBROSE, among others, and none will fit anywhere except I M B R U E S / G O / A E / M O R T S or S L U M B E R / O R T S / E L. But if he uses the I of A V A I L he can develop I M B U R S E D and M O R T. He does so only because

I M B U R S E D seems slightly better placed than S L U M B E R or I M B R U E S.

D A T E acquires O I W and D A T E O I W cannot make a seven-letter word on the board no matter how hard Player 2 tries. He does not succumb to the temptation of making W A D D I E or W A D E D by using the D on the bottom line. That's what I call self-discipline. Instead, he uses his O W to create O W N by using the N of F A N C Y, for then his D or T can be placed before it as well as his A over G A T E and his D beneath it. Moreover, he is left with D A T E I and his chances of making a seven-letter word or an eight-letter word by using the R, S, E or D of I M B U R S E D are very strong. Yes, I know his opponent can also do many things, especially using the D on the bottom line but he may not – and what if he does? If he wastes the bottom treble for 20 or 30 points that is his bad play and if he makes an eight-letter word then he is very, very fortunate. It is best to play the percentage game and not worry about the other player.

Player 1 has obtained S U I T O R R and is in trouble. After much cogitation he keeps the letters S T O I R and plays the U R after the G of G A T E to make G U R which takes L, U or S after it. It often happens that, between two good players, the bottom or other triple such as this is left open for several moves.

D A E T E I draws S E and no seven-letter word springs to mind but then Player 2 sees S T E A D I E D on the bottom line and, keeping this in reserve, he tries to make an eight-letter word starting and ending on triple squares. As a matter of fact I cannot see one that he can make anywhere else (maybe you can), and he is just about to settle for S T E A D I E D for 77 points when the word I D E A T E S hurtles into his mind. This will score 87 points from I D E A T E S / S O W N or 74 points from I D E A T E S / G U R S and either play will open up the top part of the board and leave the bottom line for better things. He decides against opening a third triple with I D E A T E S / G U R S although this would place the letter I two squares before the triple-word square. Somehow, having three triples open at once seems a bit too open to me, though you may call me tiny-minded. He plays I D E A T E S / S O W N for 97 points, allowing the I, D and E of I D E A T E S to await another suitable group of seven letters to create an eight-letter word.

* * * *

4
The End-Game

One can reasonably state the end-game to be the part of the game where there are about ten to fourteen letters left in the bag. Obviously the final end-game is when there are only three to five letters left but more of that later.

The end-game has more importance than is usually ascribed to it and with practice and patience you may improve it no end! I will not bore you with what to do when there are few letters left in the bag and the Q has not appeared or is on your rack and there is only one U or none left; you will have come across this problem already in your own experience and a little thought will take care of it.

If I asked you to check all the letters to see what distribution of each letter remained in the bag and/or on your opponent's rack most of you would laugh at me! Don't worry – it is not necessary. What I will ask of you is to think of what letters will assist you to form a seven- or eight-letter word and to count how many of them (or it) have already appeared on the board and/or on your rack.

The number you come up with should be compared with the original distributive number of them (or it) and the odds calculated; e.g. if you need an E and eight have appeared then there are four of them left in the bag and/or on your opponent's rack. If there are thirteen letters left in the bag then this should be added to the letters on your opponent's rack making twenty in all. Therefore, of those twenty letters there are four that will serve your purpose, so it is a four to one shot. These odds should be grabbed at this stage for we are no longer in the middle-game when two to one was the longest shot you should take. Here, in the end-game, five to one is about the maximum odds you should risk. In this case you should exchange your odd letter and trust to luck.

The reason why I advocate taking odds of up to five to one is because it is usually very difficult to make a seven- or eight-letter word at this stage and if you have the chance to do so, then do it! The state of the board at this stage infrequently lends itself to scores of 60/90 points and players are usually content with 10/20 points per move. Contentment is one thing but tactics are another, and it is at this period of a game that it is often won or lost because of thought or lack of it.

Perception of words on the board may show you that one or more will only take a specific letter (or two) after or before them; for example, if a word will receive an S or a D after it then a quick count-up will serve to display to you the fact that you may have the last S or D (or both) on your rack. What a golden opportunity is thrust your way! Only you can use this opening so why not use it to maximum effect? If you can obtain a seven-letter word to fit into this opening, then how much better it will be to do so than merely to use a four- or five-letter word. It is worthwhile foregoing a few points by trying to make a seven-letter word (with reasonable odds) rather than scoring 15/25 points and abusing the opening.

During this part of the game you may also see the opportunity of making a two-, three- or four-letter word which will only accept another letter on your rack. Count how many of this letter have appeared and you may discover that you hold the last one. Even if you hold one of the last two it is still worthwhile making the move. The odds against your opponent having the other survivor are probably only evens or two to one but it may still be advantageous to take the risk.

Now is the time to check the letters already played on the board; look for C, F, P, V or W and of course the big four J, Q, X and Z. There are only two of each of the letters C, F, P, V and W so it should not take you long. Whatever of these letters are absent from the board will help you to see what difficulty your opponent may have in placing them on the board. Obviously you cannot know exactly what letters your opponent has, but in time you will master the exact distribution so that when no letters are left in the bag you will know precisely what letters your opponent has on his rack.

If your opponent has a C or V or both then you may observe the few places on the board, if any, where he could use one or both, with or without a vowel on his rack; thus you can use these places yourself, leaving your opponent with a letter or letters unusable at the end of the game. It may seen unprofitable for you to make low scores by going in these one or two places, but remember that the letters left unusable on your opponent's rack are of double value to you in the final scores. Also, you will often create for yourself the opportunity of slowly using your letters to maximum effect while knowing that your opponent has been rendered helpless.

The use of a blank or an S during the end-game is dealt with in the next chapter.

We must consider your position with the last seven or so letters left on your rack. It is of no use looking for the best scoring opportunity with some of them and ignoring the rest. You must diligently work out the various combinations of letters to make all the possible words on your rack. Then take each word or letter-combination one at a time and see in how many places you can insert it on the board and what points it will score for you. Consider whether you may go out in two or three or four moves and whether your opponent is likely to allow you such grace. Try to spot alternative positions where you can go out in two moves if possible, and even if they do not score so highly for you as going out in three or more moves then stick to them, for you will obtain the points value doubled, in effect, of the letters your opponent is caught with.

Try to get rid of your high-scoring letters first of all as your opponent will frequently have calculated some of the letters you are left with and will be trying to catch you with them. If you have a C or a V or both then look for the one or two places where you may use it or them, and dive in quickly so as to get them off your rack, so that you do not suffer the double penalty of having them deducted from your total and also added to your opponent's total. Do not hope to be able to place your letters where you want in the order you wish for, as your opponent will often forestall your wishes.

Sometimes you will actually score only a few points on the board with your last moves but your final total will be more than it might have been because you have rid yourself of letters that would have been deducted from your score.

Figure 7a

33

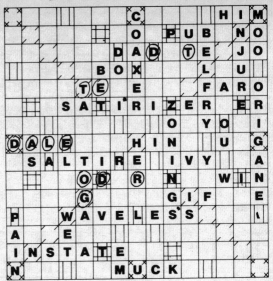

Figure 7b

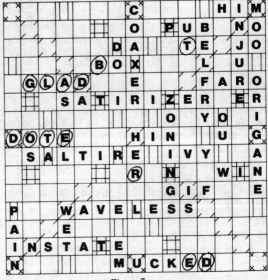

Figure 7c

You will occasionally be faced with a choice of blocking your opponent's placement of a sticky letter or scoring more highly elsewhere; if it is his only placement then block it and you will score more highly still!

Here are some examples of end-game play. In each case illustration (a) shows the state of the game when we join it and illustrations (b) and (c) the finished game after the alternative endings have been played.

Figure 7(a) shows the state of a game where Player 1 has scored 393 and has B R O T T E D left on his rack, and Player 2 has a score of 426 and Q G A D D L E remaining. There are no letters left in the bag as Player 2's last move was S A L T I R E / H E, taking the last seven available letters.

Now Player 1 knows that Player 2 must have picked up the Q in the last seven letters without a U as all the U's have been played with only the U of P U B permitting the placement of a Q and A to make Q U A / A E.

By counting the eight A's on the board Player 1 realises that his opponent has an A to go with the Q and only one place to use them. By using a B and T to make B U T / G E he can ensure that Player 2 is stymied with the Q, thus giving a twenty-point edge in Player 1's favour. He needs it! He is 33 points behind.

Before jumping in with his B U T / T E he checks to see if he can make a bonus word with his B R O T T E D. He cannot but he must also search to find the highest scoring places for his letters. He sees that his B is useful to make B O X / B E T or B O X / B O T and thinks that he need only create U T / T E to spoil Player 2's Q placement, retaining his B for better use. He also notices that he has D E B T O R to place before the S of S A L T I R E, though for only 12 points. Finally he observes D O T E / O S / T A / E L for 25 points and has to stop himself from doing it right away. He plays U T / T E for only 4 points. Scores 397 – 426.

Player 2 is appalled but places the Q at the end of his rack and looks to see what he can best do with the other six letters. He understands that Player 1 will now maximise the use of his letters with all the time and all the moves he needs available to him! He mentally deducts 20 points from his score and fearfully realises that there are now only 9 points between them.

His best move seems to be D A L E / A S / L A / E L for 25 points and he grabs it. He should have hesitated over whether G A L E might not have been better than D A L E, leaving him with D D Q rather than G D Q. If he has, he would have played G A L E instead of D A L E for the D is more pointsworthy than the G. His score is now 451 and he is 54 points ahead, subject to the Q.

Player 1 is upset for he was counting on D O T E / O S / T A / E L's 25 points to help him in his dire state. Now he is 34 points behind after accounting for the Q. He thinks he had better check the letters placeable before O X to see if he should use it now or whether he can safely make another move like T O / O D / I D for 16 points without the O X being used up. The letters B, C, F, H, L, P, S and V are all safely out except his last B. He plays T O / O D / I D for 16 points and as he does so he realises he can later play his T to make E L T / T O D. His score is now 413, only 18 points behind.

Player 2 sees that T O / O D / I D has opened up the word T O G A for 12 points and he could then score 7 points with D A D below the top centre triple-word square. These 19 points would mean that Player 1 would have to score 37 points to draw level with him. As Player 1 only has four letters left it seems unlikely but if Player 2 plays T O G A for 12 points might not Player 1 then use up all his four letters to score 28 points which would win him the game by two points with Player 2 caught with the D as well as the Q? He could play G A D for only 10 points but then Player 1 would only need 28 points with four letters to win.

What a quandary! Player 2 ponders a trifle then plays T O G A making his score 463.

Player 1 doesn't like the look of it but search as he may he cannot find a better move than B O X / B E T for 17 points. Total 430.

Player 2 sees E L D / D O D for 9 points but is unsure of D O D and decides to accept D A D for 7 safe points, total 470.

Player 1 is now 20 points behind after taking the Q into account and scours the board; he sees R E / R A T for 10 points or T A / T E for 8 points plus H E R for 6 points making 14 points in total. He cannot find better and plays the two moves for 8 and 6 points.

With the Q's 10 points the final scores are Player 1 : 454 points and Player 2 : 460 points.

Although Player 1 scored 61 points from 393 to 454 and Player 2 only scored 34 points from 426 to 460 the leeway was a little too much for Player 1 to make up. But the example shows how Player 1 maximised his end-game by thinking of the Q.

Let us now go back to see what might have happened if Player 1 had not blocked the use of the Q. Player 1 has 393 points and Player 2 has 426 points. This alternative ending can be seen on Figure 7c.

Player 1 can score 25 points with D O T E / O S / T A / E L but this leaves him with three consonants, B, R and T. The only place he can go out with B, R and T is by making B R A T for 12 points by using the A of S A T I R I Z E R. He counts up mentally; the 25 points would make him 418 to Player 2's 426 with Player 2 having one move before the 12 points with B R A T are scored. Player 2 will have to make Q U A / A E for 14 points, bringing his score to 440.

Player 1 will then score the 12 points for B R A T making his total 430 points and catching Player 2 with five letters left on his rack. Without working out what letters they are Player 1 realises that they must total at least 5 points. This invaluable 5 points doubled would level the scores between them and if only one of the letters is worth two points then Player 1 will win the game. He mentally starts off with the first two-point consonant which is D and sees only one D on the board. With the D on his own rack it means Player 2 must have not one but two D's on his rack so Player 1 can win the game.

Player 1 realises that the only way he can lose is if Player 2 stops him from making B R A T. This is unlikely unless Player 2 has worked out what letters Player 1 possesses and also what move Player 1 has in mind after making D O T E / O S / T A / E L for 25 points. Even if Player 2 has done this and spoils B R A T by playing G L A D / A S / D A for 20 points this 20 points will be nullified by Player 1 when using the U of P U B to make R U T / T E and saving his B to make B O X or D A B for 12 or 9 points respectively. The Q will be left on Player 2's rack with D and E.

So Player 1 plays D O T E / O S / T A / E L for 25 points, making his score 418 to Player 2's 426 points.

Player 2 has Q G A D D L E and there is no way he can see to win. Let us presume that he works out Player 1's three remaining letters B, R and T and decides to spoil B R A T with the main intention, not of winning, but of maximising his own score and ending up with more than 432 (add 14 to 426 for Q U A / A E; subtract 8 for the letters left on the rack). He plays G L A D / A S / D A for 20 points, totalling 446.

Player 1 has 418 points and the letters B, R and T and knows that Q reduces the deficit to only 8 points between them. Instead of playing R U T / T E for 5 points he realises he can play U R / R E or U T / T E for 4 points each so that he can then use the T or R respectively to score more than 1 point. He scans the board to see where an R or a T can score best for him and the most he can see is 6 points by making H E R in the middle of the board (H E T would have done also). He plays U T / T E for 4 points, totalling 422.

Player 2 has 446 and Q, D and E. He realises that there are only 4 points between them after taking the Q into account and Player 2 has B and R left. He is fairly sure that Player 1 will now take his time because he is stuck with the Q and that Player 1 will probably make B O X rather than D A B with his next move. Player 2 can only score 8 points with H E E D, 9 points with D A / D I E / E E, or 7 points with I D using the I of S A L T I R E and keeping his E to score 6 points with E A S using the A of G L A D. Therefore 13 points is the most he can score with his E and D, making 17 points between the players and Player 1 to score with his B and R. He sees Player 1's possible 12 points with B O X and possible 6 points with H E R, totalling 18 points.

Player 2 then realises that his E D would go well after B O X, which is likely to be made by Player 1. BOXED would score him 15 points making him the winner by one point! But how can he pass his turn without making Player 1 suspicious and playing his B and R together for 5 points to win the game there and then. He could play T E / E D / I D by using the T and I of S A L T I R E knowing that Player 1 would successfully challenge E D. But would not player 1 then realise that Player 2 had deliberately done that? Who knows? Just then Player 2 sees M U C K E D for 17 points and places his E D after M U C K before he gets a headache!

So Player 2 has 463 points and the dead Q on his rack, Player 1 has 422 points and B and R and has to score 22 points with the B and R to win the game. He can't. He plays B for B O X and 12 points and the R for H E R and 6 points totalling 440 points. The 10 points for the Q must be added to Player 1's score making 450 points, and deducted from Player 2's score, making 453 points. If only B R A T had not been spoilt!

These different ways of ending the game should show you how a little thought can make all the difference between winning and losing.

* * * *

In figure 8 we have reached a stage where Player 1 is 375 with V I N G L E S on his rack and Player 2 is 344 and it is his move with P L A N J O N on his rack. There are 5 letters left in the bag.

Player 2 is lagging by 31 points and can see that both blanks and three S's have gone. He observes that there is room for a seven-letter word starting with any vowel over the last S of H A I R L E S S, an eight-letter word starting with the D of R A D I A L E S and only taking the U after the D or an eight-letter word ending with the I or C of U R I C, which he dismisses as too remote; the same remoteness applies to a nine-letter word starting with U N at the top of the board.

He would like to get the last S but Player 1 has seven letters on his rack and there are only 5 letters left in the bag, so the chances are that Player 1 has the S. Even if he kept L O A N, a reasonable grouping but not a good one, and exchanged P N J for the three letters in the bag, the odds would be against him getting suitable letters to make a bonus word in the positions described. He can make little use of the high-scoring J so he decides to score 27 points with A T O P. He dislikes being left with L N N J but feels this is his best move in the circumstances (Figure 8b). This makes him 371 to Player 1's 375. He gets Y O E to join his L N N J.

Player 1 is fairly sure U R I C is an adjective only and not a noun so it

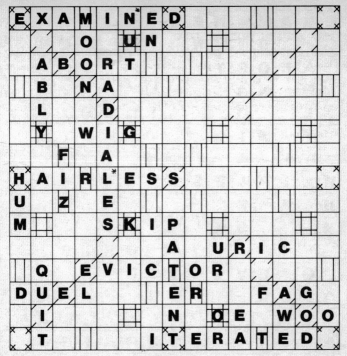

Figure 8a

won't take his S even if he changes the V for a letter which would, if he were lucky, make him a bonus word. He too can see that the blanks are out but he has the last S. He can only see three of the Big four and wonders if his opponent has the J or if it is one of the two letters left in the bag. Even J I N G L E S would not help him!

He is only 4 points ahead and getting worried. He would like to use the V or the V and G and make a possible usable opening for himself but he can't. As he has an I or an E to go over the S of H A I R L E S S he reasons he has a possible chance of obtaining two reasonable letters to join his I N L E S for a bonus word if he changes his V and G for the last two letters. Also, they will provide little help for his opponent, especially the V. If his opponent takes the last two letters he will know that they are V and G and might be able to block any chance of the V being used. He exchanges and receives T and H.

39

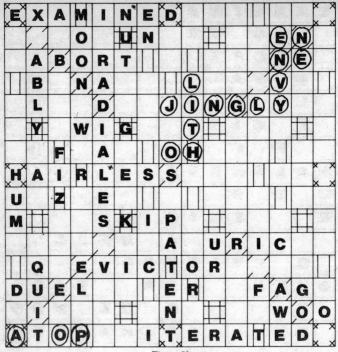

Figure 8b

Player 2 now knows his opponent must have the last S. His highest scoring move is E N J O Y / E S for 18 points, leaving him with L N plus the last two letters from the bag. He is afraid that his opponent may then go out by playing a bonus word, containing the S which would also, make E N J O Y S. He will be caught with L N plus another two letters and lose the game. If he makes O S by placing his O above the last S of H A I R L E S S his opponent may still go out by using a bonus word starting with one of the many letters placeable above O S. If his opponent does not or does not use the O S then he can make O S / J E N N Y or J E N N Y / O Y for 27 or 38 points respectively. If his opponent uses the O S in any way then such use may provide him with a good scoring position for his J or Y or both of them. At least his opponent will have to take the last letter from the bag whatever move he makes. He plays O S for 2 points. The scores are now 373 to 375.

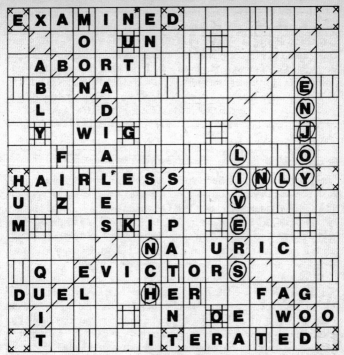

Figure 8c

Player 1 has H I N T L E S and is only two points ahead. He cannot make a seven-letter word from H I N T L E S nor an eight-letter word by using the R or I or C of U R I C. The N A at the top of the board does not help him, nor can the O of O S or the U R starting with the U of U R I C. He knows F A G will accept an E after it but cannot make an eight-letter word ending with E O. He suddenly sees L I T H E N S and wonders if L I T H E N is an archaic verb connected to L I T H E. Probably not. He decides to play L I T H / O H for 20 valuable points and picks up the V to accompany his N E S. The scores are 395 to 373.

Player 2 now feels the draught. he has L N N J Y E G, is 22 points behind and his 38-point J E N N Y / O Y was just a dream. He looks around for the awkward letters like C and V and realises that Player 1 must have the last V. Ruefully he also knows that he has the last S. The only place he can see for the V is V A N / A I, placing the A above the I of

41

I T E R A T E D, and by counting the nine A's gone he knows his opponent has a problem with the V. He is not worried about the I of L I T H for he will use it himself with J I N G L E or J I N G L Y. Although J I N G L Y scores more than J I N G L E this does not greatly concern him for he is more perturbed that his opponent may use the E of J I N G L E to get his V out. Also, J I N G L Y leaves him with N E instead of N Y from J I N G L E. The N E can make G E N or Y E N or Y E / E N with the G or Y respectively of J I N G L Y or the E can usefully make Z E E / R E for 14 points if his opponent stops GEN or YEN or YE/EN. He plays J I N G L Y for 34 points. 407 to 395.

Player 1 is now 12 points behind. Strive as he may his best move is E N V Y for 20 points, leaving him the with S. 415 to 407.

Player 2 is 8 points behind and must not let his opponent use the S so he has to search for 8 points with his E N. He sees 12 points with N E O / F A G E but is fairly sure that N E O is an unallowable prefix. He then observes E N / E N for 8 points by using the E of E N V Y and almost settles for it to win by two points by catching Player 1 with the S when he mentally kicks himself for nearly missing E N / N E / N E with the same E for ten points. He plays this and the final scores are 418 to 414.

Player 2 seems lucky to have won this game after being 31 points behind with five letters left in the bag, and having P L A N J O N to player 1's V I N G L E S, but you will have observed that his luck was slight compared with his skill in the end-game. Some of you may think that Player 1 took a foolish risk in exchanging his V and G to try and obtain a bonus word. Let's go back and see a different story. Figure 8c.

Player 1 has V I N G L E S and is 375 to Player 2's 371 with two letters left in the bag. His best move is L I V E R S / E V I C T O R S for 22 points and not G I V E R S / E V I C T O R S for 23 points as by keeping N G instead of N L he can later play the N G with the I of E V I C T O R S to make I N G or with the I of L I V E R S to make G I N. Also he has a slight chance of placing the G above U R near U R I C to create G U R and G E T and T I if he picks up the last T. The score is now 397 to 371, with Player 1 acquiring T H to join his N G.

Player 2, with L O E N N J Y, is now 26 points behind with no letters left in the bag and his opponent has only four letters on his rack. Now it is vital for him to work out all or most of Player 2's letters for him to have the best chance of winning. Let us presume he does so and sees that Player 1's best moves are G E T / G U R / T I for 18 points and I N C H / N A / H E R for 25 points and out! There is not much he can do about it as Player 1 can also play his N H with the I of L I V E R S to make H I N and also go out!

Player 2 can only see J O L L Y or J E L L Y for 27 points by using the L of L I V E R S, leaving him with E N N or O N N. If he plays J E L L Y then he could go out in two moves for 33 points by then using his O N N to make N O N E with the E of J E L L Y. He is fairly sure Player 2 will first make I N C H / N A / H E R for 25 points, making the score difference 51 points. His 33 points in two moves will reduce the deficit to 18 points and the G and T caught on Player 1's rack will further reduce it to 12 points. But Player 2 still loses! He could play N Y L O N / L O / I N for 23 points, by using the L I of L I V E R S and leaving himself with with J E but the J E is then almost useless. Then he sees that by playing L N with the I of LIVERS he could make LIN for 4 points, awaiting his further construction of ENJOY/LINO for 31 points. Total 35 points and still not enough.

Further concentration by Player 2 produces I N L Y, by using N L Y and the I of L I V E R S, for 8 points, followed by E N J O Y for 31 points, totalling 39 points. Better but still failing by 6 points. His only hope is that Player 1 does not see I N C H / N A / H E R for 25 points or plays G E T / G U R / T I first for 18 points. He plays I N L Y for 8 points.

Player 1 has worked out his possible plays and has seen that Player 2 must have the J, but has not bothered to work out Player 2's other letters (if he had it would make no difference here). He sees he has only one good place for his H N so he plays I N C H / N A / H E R for 25 points.

Player 2 cannot block G E T / G U R / T I without using his valuable O so he resigns himself to defeat and plays E N J O Y for 31 points and out. The final score is 413 to 419.

So in illustration 8c player 1 scrapes home by 6 points by not taking a chance of making a bonus word with I N L E S plus the last two letters (unknown). The odds against him were too high.

* * * *

Player 2 has scored 376 and the letters on his rack are F L Y W V D L; Player 1 has only 335 and S T R A N G B and it is his turn. There are seven letters left in the bag; the state of the board is shown in Figure 9a.

41 points behind, Player 1 feels desperate. He can see his N G fitting nicely after the I of Q U A I L but doesn't think S T R A B can be positioned in any way around I N G to make a word. I don't either. He realises that the V of V E N D O R S and the I and L of Q U A I L are the only letters to assist him in the formation of an eight-letter word and that his opponent may very quickly use one of them, probably the I or L or both.

He decides to go through the alphabet to see what letters will assist him in making an eight-letter word if he exchanges the B and is surprised to discover C, D, E, F, G, L, P, R, T V, W and Y as assistants. These make TRACINGS, TRADINGS, ANGRIEST/RANGIEST/STEARING/

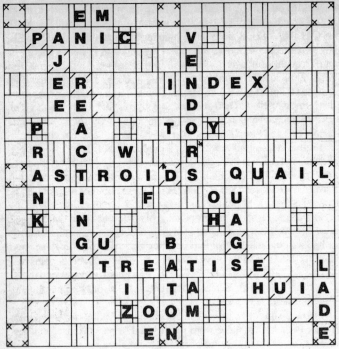

Figure 9a

GANISTER/ASTRINGE, STRANGLE, STRAFING, GRATINGS,
STARLING, PARTINGS, STARRING, STARTING, STARVING,
STRAWING, STRAYING.

He checks the letters on the board and finds that of the twelve usable
letters only seven are still available for use; however, two L's are unused so
that makes a total of nine usable letters. Seven letters in the bag and seven
letters on his opponent's rack! He has nine chances out of fourteen to
make his bonus word of eight letters .If his opponent lets him!

At this stage of the game a better than even chance of getting a bonus
word must be grabbed, especially when you have the last S and are 41
points behind. Player 1 exchanges his B.

Player 2 can see the openness of the letters I and L of Q U A I L but is
more concerned with his lack of a vowel with F L Y W V D L. He can see
F I L L Y for 13 points by using the I of Q U A I L and F L E W for 20 points

44

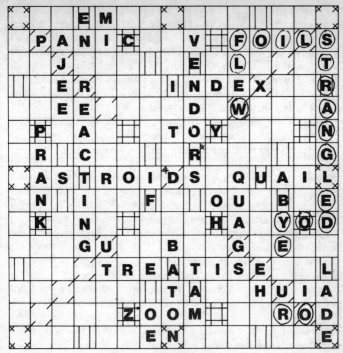

Figure 9b

by using the E of I N D E X. He realises that F I L L Y will probably spoil his opponent's chances of making an eight-letter word ending with or containing the L of Q U A I L. He then thinks that the F of F I L L Y can take an A after it and allow an eight-letter word ending in A L and decides to plump for the higher score of 20 points with F L E W. The score is 396 to 335. Figure 9b.

Player 1 gets an E to make S T R A N G E. He thinks that his opponent has trouble because he used three consonants to make F L E W but rejoices that the openings were not blocked. He chooses S T R A N G L E for 60 points instead of S T E A R I N G for 65 points so as to stop his opponent from possibly scoring highly with his next move by using the top right-hand triple square. The score is now 395 to 396.

Player 2's YVDL gets OIO to make YVDLOIO. He is very worried now to be only one point ahead with his opponent having only four letters left on his rack. He doesn't want to be caught with the V or Y or both and can see V L Y, I V Y, V O I D, V I O L and O V O I D but cannot place them on the board. He thinks about many possible moves and finally narrows them down to Y O D / S T R A N G L E D for 20 points, leaving him with V I O L, or H A L O I D / S T R A N G L E D for 23 points leaving him with V O Y. He selects Y O D / S T R A N G L E D for the smaller score of 20 points because his V I O L can go out by making O L I V E with the E of L A D E if he gets the chance. Score now 416 to 395.

Player 1 now takes the time to work out Player 2's remaining letters. It is not a very hard task. The V and the L come very quickly as he knew about the second L before. He then sees that V I O L can go out with O L I V E for 9 points, so he has to score 33 points with three of his letters R O B E and use the B amongst them as he cannot find a place to go out with R O B E / B O R E for 8 points to win the game (catching Player 2 with V I O L).

He starts looking for the places usable by Player 2 with his V and any of the letters I O L. He finds O V A twice by using the A of Q U A I L or the A of S T R A N G L E D and finds O V E R by using the E R at the top left-hand corner of the board. He can play R O D / U R / I O for 18 points by using the D of L A D E and thereby spoiling O L I V E and forcing his opponent to use O V in the next move. The 18 points thus gained will reduce the deficit to 3 points, probably then rising to 13 points when his opponent plays O V A using the A of Q U A I L as his highest and best scoring move. Player 1 can then go out for 10 points or more with B E to win the game by catching his opponent with L I. He plays R O D / U R / I O for 18 points, and the score is 413 to 416.

Player 2 has been busy thinking and has worked out the B E left on Player 1's rack and sees B E / E S for 12 points or B E / U R E for 10 points, winning the game for Player 1 if Player 2 plays O V A for the maximum score of 10 points. He vainly looks around for better and only sees F O I L S for 16 points leaving him with the V. this will mean that Player 1 must score 12 points by using his B and E at leisure while Player 2 is stuck with his V. He sees that Player 1 can do this as he espies A B Y for 11 points by using the A of Q U A I L and the Y of Y O D. Although he will lose the game he will at least maximise his own score by playing F O I L S. He plays it for 16 points and the scores are 432 to 413.

Player 1 heaves a sigh of relief as he was afraid Player 2 would see something he had missed. He realises that the true difference in scores is 11 points because of the V and quickly sees A B Y E for 12 points to win the game. Then he stops his fingers moving towards the letters and reflects that he can probably score more by playing his B for A B Y for 11 points and then playing his E elsewhere. Elsewhere only means 7 points by placing between the K of P R A N K and the N of R E A C T I N G. He plays

B for A B Y and 11 points and then the E for A B Y E and 9 points. After taking the V into account the final scores are Player 1 : 437, Player 2 : 428.

This was an exceptionally fine game for Player 1 to win after being 41 points behind with only seven letters left. He was lucky inasmuch as his opponent had bad letters on his rack with F L Y W V D L, but it was really his skill in the end-game that won it for him.

5

The S and the Blank

There are only four S's but next to the two blanks they are the most powerful letters in the game. So frequently do I encounter players using an S for 10 to 25 points without a qualm that I shudder to think of it! An S is such a precious commodity that it should have its proper value appreciated lest it fall into the fingers of an ignorant possessor.

I will state categorically that an S should not be used for a score of less than 30 points and then only most reluctantly. You should keep an S on your rack for three or four moves if necessary, in the hope of scoring 60 to 90 points with it. Normally you will make such a score during the period of the three or four moves by using the S in a seven- or eight-letter word.

By 'normally' I mean making one's moves in such a way as to retain on one's rack the most likely combination of letters to accompany the S from the letters picked up in exchange for the letters used on the board. This may not be normal for you but kindly make it so!

Groupings of letters that should be retained with an S are:

A I T	A N T E	G E A R
A N T	A N T I	N E A R
A R E	C A N E	N E A T
E A T	D A N T	R A I N
E N T	D A T E	R A N G
I D E	D E A N	R A T E
I N G	D E A R	R E I N
I R E	D E N T	R E N G
R E D	D I N T	R E N T
R E T	D I R E	R I N G
T E D	G A T E	T I R E
	G A I T	T R E E

By shuffling the above castings around with an S you need only a little luck to pick up the letters necessary to make a seven-letter word. Try it!

After retaining any of the above three- or four-letter groupings with an S you will often obtain the letters needed to make one or more seven-letter words appear on your rack. Sometimes you will be unlucky and then you must try again with the best possible three, four or five letters on your rack plus the S to get a letter or letters to make a bonus word. At the same time you will be scoring points with the letters you are using, though of course not as many as if you had used the S and/or the retained letters.

For example, suppose you have S E A R C L Y. You do not use CARES,

SCARY OR CLAYS but you try to utilise C L Y (which is a word) with an A or an O on the board to make C L A Y or L A C Y or C O L Y, thus keeping S E A R. If you cannot do so then use C R Y and retain S E A L. Again, say you possess S A T N P E B. Never use PANTS or BATES or BANES or PANES. Retain S A T N E if you can by using the P and the B to create P U B or B A P with the appropriate loose vowel on the board. By keeping S A T N E you have a very good chance of picking up two letters to make a seven-letter word, e.g. I and D, I and G, I and L, I and M, I and R, I and T, E and L, E and M, E and N, E and T, R and D, R and C, R and E, R and G, R and H, R and K, R and L, R and N, R and R, R and S, R and U, R and V, R and W, to name but a few. The seven-letter words they make are STAINED, SEATING, ENTAILS, INMATES, NASTIER, SATINET, LEANEST, MEANEST, NEATENS, NEATEST, STANDER, CANTERS, EASTERN, STRANGE, THENARS, TANKERS, ANTLERS, TANNERS, ERRANTS, TRANSES, SAUNTER, TAVERNS, WANTERS.

I have just given you some fairly awkward examples and you have followed them quite easily. How much easier it must be when you possess S E A N T I Y! Here you use the Y (if you can) or, if not, you exchange it for another letter as any of the letters B, C, D, E, G, I, L, M, O, R, S, T U or V (among others) will make a seven-letter word for you. The words are BESTAIN/BESAINT, CINEAST/CANIEST, INSTEAD, ETESIAN, S E A TING/TEASING/TANGIEST/EASTING/INGATES/ISATINE, ENTAILS/SALIENT/TENAILS/STANIEL, INMATES/ TAMINES, ATONIES, NASTIER etc, TANSIES, SATINET, SINUATE, VAINEST/ NAIVEST. There are also probably one or more letters usable on the board that will make an eight-letter word; for example, a loose I will create VANITIES if you pick up a V, a loose O will make SEDATION with a D, an A will form SANITATE with a T, a P will create PANTILES with an L and so on.

What if you have S T R E N D V? would you make VENTS? Please don't! Here you must get rid of the V (an awkward customer) and another consonant, for it is too dangerous to keep S T R E N D for it only has one vowel. If you cannot do this with the condition of the board as it is then use V E N D and retain S T R, for the chances are that you will obtain one or two vowels in the four letters you add to your rack. But it would be better to keep S T E R N and exchange D V.

Say you possessed S T E A D P H. Here the word D A T E S is a useful group of letters and it is usually possible to place the letters P H so as to form H A P, H E P, H O P, H I P or H U P on the board. If not then it is worthwhile exchanging the P H for another two letters rather than using the P or H alone.

If S T I R E A J were on your rack then it would be a golden opportunity to use the J alone or exchange it for another letter because A, B, D, F, G, H, I, L, M, N, P, R, S, T or W will all fit in to make ATRESIA/ ASTERIA, BAITERS, ASTRIDE/STAIRED/STAIDER/TIRADES, FAIREST, TRIAGES/STRIGAE, GAITERS/STAGIER, HASTIER/SHERIAT, AIRIEST/IRISATE, REALIST/RETAILS/SALTIER/SATIRE, MAISTER/MASTIER, RETAINS etc. PASTIER etc. SATIRES/ TIRASSE, TASTIER/ARTISTE/ATTIRES or WAITERS. I cannot resist stating the obvious, SATIRE has 85 chances out of 93, subject to the letters on the board, to make a seven-letter word, quite apart from the other opportunities of creating an eight-letter word with the letters available on the board at the time.

You now realise how precious an S is. Then how much more valuable is a blank? The question is best answered by saying that a blank should never be used for less than 50 points unless you have both blanks or you are at the end of a game and must use it in the best way possible to score most aptly in the circumstances.

Would that I could adequately extol the praises of a blank. I regret that I am incapable of doing so as the sight of one on my rack makes me judder with joy – the joy of knowing I have a 50-100 point score coming up the joy of knowing that I can juggle with my other letters and create a seven-letter word (usually in one to three moves).

I may not be able to express fully my love of blanks, but at least I can reveal the horror I feel when I see someone playing one for only 15 or 30 points. I am revolted to see it placed on the board in such a pitiful state, rendered impotent of the powers it possesses by an unwitting depositor.

The blank should be treasured on your rack for as long as it takes to make a seven-letter or eight-letter word or at least score 50 points with it. Sometimes one can retain it for five or six moves if the letters run against one. This is unfortunate but it occurs very rarely, as also does the chance of using a triple-word square with another triple-word square (a nine-timer) by using the blank in your custody. Either can happen so this is a fair representation of the law of averages.

Should you get both blanks at once then beware of keeping both of them if one will score you at least 35 points. It is better to do this than to hang on to both hoping for a nine-timer or an easier way of making a seven-letter word. By using one blank for 35 points of thereabouts you may also make an opening for yourself to use the other blank at the beginning and/or the end of the word you have placed on the board.

Should you get a blank or an S during the end-game (when there are ten to fourteen letters left in the bag) then you should scan the board to see what openings are available on which you can tack a seven-letter word.

Should there be none, then make two openings to give yourself the best chance in case your opponent closes one or the letters fitting onto such openings are restricted in number or choice. Work out what letter or letters you need to create a seven-letter word on your rack, count such letters already played on the board and see how many are left available to you if they are not on your opponent's rack. Then play to get the letter or letters by making openings with the letter or letters you have, regardless of the small scores you are making. You may not get one but your blank or S means that you must try.

Sometimes blanks and S's have the effrontery to hide themselves until the end-game arrives and are not usable for bonus words. This defies description but happens to all of us at one time or another and there is nothing I can say to assist a situation where the last six to ten letters contain a blank which scores lowly or not at all. It is hell!

You should be aware of the likelihood of your opponent having a blank and/or an S at the end of the game and take steps to neutralise or minimise the opportunities or openings available for him or her to spring a bonus score on you at this stage.

6
General Play and Hints

Now I have a licence for rambling – so let us elide the R from RAMBLING and consider AMBLING. It is a nice seven-letter word but if you had LAMBING or BLAMING viewable on your rack would you continue to think and so discover AMBLING? Perhaps not, but you should, since it is the only anagram which will accept F, G, H or R before it to enable it to be scored again. If it is made into HAMBLING or RAMBLING it can be scored yet again if an S or B is placed respectively before them.

This is an example of the need not to be content with the first or second anagram you see on your rack but to rearrange the letters again and again to try to produce the most receptive word. Sometimes one is lucky enough to obtain a word like RAPPING which will accept C, D, F, T or W before it without much ado, but more often than not one has to juggle the letters for better benefit.

TIARAED is a word some will spot and know or essay in hope, without considering RADIATE, which will take an E before it or S or D after it, while others may only see DEMERIT and ignore MERITED, which can attract an E before it.

LIT?ERS will form STILLER, LEISTER, REALIST, TILLERS, LITTERS, FILTERS, TESTRIL and others. Which one would you use so as to obtain the utmost future benefit? Yes, LITTERS will take C, F, G or S before it to rescore most fruitfully.

TANGLER is a word you might jump at to use, without realising that TRANGLE exists and accepts S before and S or D after it, while the words ALERTING or INTEGRAL or RELATING are not further useful though TRIANGLE will take D or S after it.

Oddly enough RATLINE/RELIANT/ENTRAIL/LATRINE/TRENIAL/RETINAL is an anagrammatical flop in the sense described above, but how useful it is to know these anagrams to enable one to pick that which is best usable or the only one which can be fitted on the board.

Seven-letter words containing the letters ING are often not used to their best advantage. Too frequently a player will spot a seven-letter word ending in ING and look no farther. Sometimes there is no need to look farther but if there is, anagrams can often be more useful. It is not realised how many seven-letter words which end in ING are anagrams of other words.

TEARING is frequently encountered in Scrabble and its alternatives or some of them are not realised or seen for their true usefulness. Consider GRANITE, INGRATE, TANGIER – they can be utilised to better effect on various occasions. SEATING/TEASING/INGATES/INGESTA/GATINGS/SIGNATE/TANGIES/TSIGANE/EASTING are 9 anagrams but which is the most useful? Either EATINGS or EASTING for they will take B, H, S or F and R respectively before them. RAILING and DIALING make GLAIRIN/LAIRING and GLIADIN respectively, which can be most useful dependent on the letters acceptable at specific openings on the board.

READING forms DEARING or GRADINE while NEARING makes GRANNIE and REARING gives GRAINER. CALORIE is also COALIER or LORICAE.

Strangely, ADORING can be replaced by IDORGAN, RETTING by GITTERN, REINING by NIGRINE, RESTING by STINGER, TIERING by TIGRINE or IGNITER.

If, having considered all the alternatives, you decide that your best bet is a word ending in ING, remember that such words are often nouns and can therefore receive an S to pluralise them. Just when this is allowable depends on each particular word's meaning or meanings in the dictionaries.

It is most important to see all the anagrams on your rack so that you are able to consider which one should be placed where it will do either the most good or the least harm to the game at that particular stage. If there is a triple-word square available which will only take a specific letter or letters of which there are still some unused, then how much better to position your anagram in another place where it will score almost as much as by using the triple-word square.

So often does the opportunity present itself for you to score 10 or 20 points fewer in one place and leave the higher scoring place open for better use that it is vital to have an anagrammatical muscle that can be exercised frequently.

Let us take the following examples:

For the sake of celerity and simplicity we will start with TRAINER positioned as an opening word so that an S may be placed before it, and the next word to appear on the opposing rack is GANNETS which can score 101 with GANNETS/STRAINER. But GANNETS will not accept a letter before or after it.

If, however, we use the I of TRAINER to make ANTIGENS this will only score 86 points. The A, E, N's and S may all be used to start or be included in eight-letter words while the G, A, N and E of GANNETS could only be used to start eight-letter words.

Figure 10

The A and N of TRAINER cannot be included in eight-letter words but are replaced by identical letters in ANTIGENS, while the T of TRAINER is also left available for similar use, which would not have been the case with GANNETS.

For the sake of 15 points difference the game would be better played with ANTIGENS.

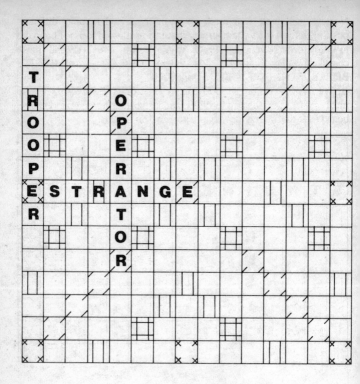

Figure 11

Here we will start with STRANGE, placed so as to take an E before it on the triple-word square. If the next word playable on the board were TROOPER then this and ESTRANGE would score 107 points.

Should we rearrange TROOPER to include the A of STRANGE, however, we could create OPERATOR for only 90 points.

The T, R and O's of TROOPER may be utilised to start eight-letter words and TROOPER may be pluralised; the O, P, E and R of OPERATOR may be used to start or be included in eight-letter words, leaving the S of STRANGE available for good use and OPERATOR may also be pluralised. Only the N of STRANGE will be nullified for use in an eight-letter word by the placement of OPERATOR for the R in STRANGE is replaced by the last R of OPERATOR.

For the loss of only 17 points it is far preferable to USE OPERATOR.

Now we will look at a made-up board contrived to offer different possibilities and show you how they should be evaluated so as to allow you to implement techniques which would permit the best and most constructive play. Figure 12a shows the board with the words IMITATE, BREAK, TANK, ARTY, BE, YO and OUR.

We now receive the word SILENCE or LICENSE on our rack and must consider how to use it fruitfully, not dash headlong to jam it onto the board as if the letters may disappear from our fingers.

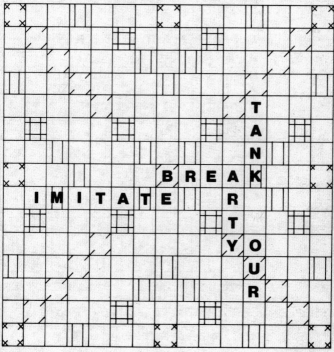

Figure 12a

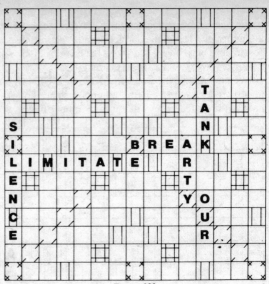

Figure 12b

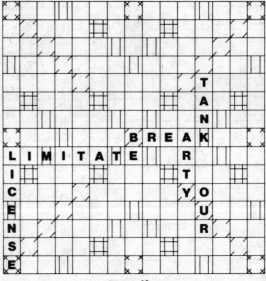

Figure 12c

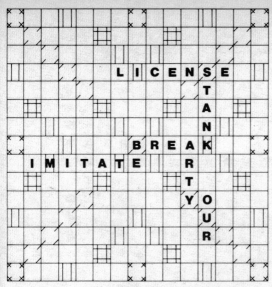

Figure 12d

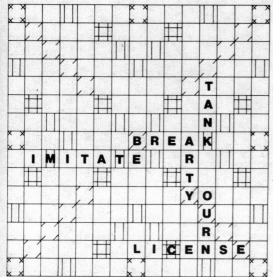

Figure 12e

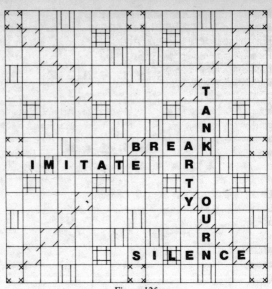

Figure 12f

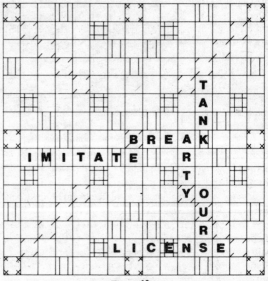

Figure 12g

Figure 12b :	SILENCE/LIMITATE	scores 96 points
Figure 12c :	LICENSE/LIMITATE	scores 90 points
Figure 12d :	LICENSE/STANK	scores 88 points
Figure 12e :	LICENSE/OURN	scores 84 points
Figure 12f :	SILENCE/OURN	scores 76 points
Figure 12g :	LICENSE/OURS	scores 65 points

We have a scoring range of 65 to 96 points, but more importantly we have to decide what is the best move in the circumstances and must consider several factors. Only an L may be positioned before IMITATE and ours is the first L to appear so there are three L's left in the bag. The word SILENCE will accept D, R and S after it while LICENSE will accept D, E, R or S after it except in Figure 12c.

A little thought will show that SILENCE/LIMITATE for 96 points or LICENSE/OURN for 84 points are the best moves for future use and LICENSE is positioned so as to make two triple-word squares readily usable.

As the letters D, E, R or S may be placed after LICENSE and A, I or O under the L, with the I of LICENSE permitting the A, I or O to attain endings like AN, IN, ON, AT, IT, AS, IS or OS, it would seem that the most fruitful move is LICENSE/OURN.

I am sure that there are other moves possible, like SILENCERS/IMITATES or LICENSERS/IMITATES for 75 or 77 points respectively, so as to place the S or L one square to the right of the top middle triple-word square, but I think you will agree that figure 12e would seem to show the most constructive move.

* * * *

Even when there is only one possible word to be made from the letters on your rack, it is always most important to consider carefully where it should be placed.

In Figure 13 we have the word FOOTLES on our rack and can place it to make FOOTLES/OHO for 96 points or FOOTLES/HEART for 92 points. There is only a difference of 4 points but what a difference in play for the future.

In either option an S can be added to form FOOTLESS, but what are the chances of making high scores with the two placements?

FOOTLES/OHO will allow a further S to be added to FOOTLES if one creates a word containing an S to be placed under it. Such a word will probably utilise the double-word square to the left just under FOOTLES but not if the word has to start with an S, in which case it will not reach the next double-word square either.

With FOOTLES/HEART one could easily use JOS or ZOS to create FOOTLESS and then the resulting score would be magnificent.

It is not just when you have a seven-letter word on your rack that you must stop and consider how to use it most constructively. The same principle applies to shorter words.

For example, you wish to play the word DARE because it will make a nice score for you and it will take a D or S after it. Why not stop to consider READ (if it fits in) which will only take an S after it but A, B, D or T before it?

The above illustration is of a simple four-letter word which becomes alive with interesting possibilities once you stop to consider them, and the same is true of more other four-letter words than I am able to mention. All that is required is for you to anagrammatise them or any three-quarters of them. Once you make a habit of this then other words will sparkle with interesting possibilities.

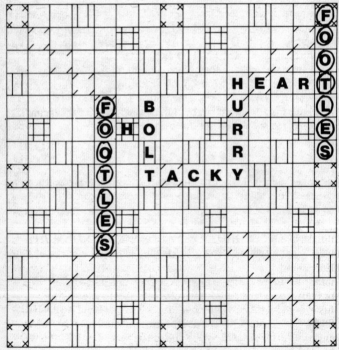

Figure 13

The following words may be utilised in the ensuing different ways:

ANTE/ETNA	(N)EAT, TAN(E), (T)ANE,
BEAR	BAR(E), BRA(E),
DEER/REED	(D)REE, RED(E),
EMIR/RIME	(M)IRE, MIR(E), RIM(E),
GORE/OGRE	(G)ORE, (O)GRE
HATE/HEAT/EATH	EAT(H), (H)ATE, (H)EAT,
	(T)HAE,
EMIT/ITEM/MITE/TIME	(E)MIT, MIT(E),
AMEN/MEAN/NAME	(A)MEN, MAN(E),
	(M)ANE,
LAME/MEAL/LEAM/MALE	LAM(E), (L)EAM, (M)ALE,
LARE/LEAR/REAL	LAR(E), (L)ARE, (L)EAR,
PARE/PEAR/RAPE/REAP	(P)ARE, PAR(E), RAP(E), (R)APE,
REDO/ROED/RODE	RED(O), ROD(E), (R)ODE, ROE(D),
DURE/RUED/RUDE	(D)URE, RUE(D), RUD(E),
LAVE/LEVA/VALE/VEAL	(L)AVE, LEV(A), (V)ALE,
ANEW/WANE/WEAN	(A)NEW, ANE(W), WAN(E),(W)ANE,

One word which requires special mention is ROT. This is because it
is an anagram of TOR and ORT. They work as follows:

(B)		(C)
(D)	(A)	(E)
(F)	(E)	(I)
(M) ORT(S)	(T) ROT (L)	TOR (N)
(P)	(S)	(R)
(S)		(S)
(T)		(T)
(W)		(Y)

Now ORT has $\frac{25}{97}$ chances of getting one of the above letters to fit it

while ROT has $\frac{36}{97}$ chances and TOR has $\frac{47}{97}$ chances. It would seem that

the letter-combination to use is TOR, or perhaps ROT because it takes a
letter in front of it and TOR does not. This is subject to the other four
letters on your rack. Strangely enough, ORT is favourite. This is because
if the letter B or M or P is played before ORT, making BORT or MORT
or PORT, then these four-letter words will take the letters A before the
first two and S before the last one to create ABORT and AMORT and
SPORT respectively. Thus the word-structure on the board would be
enhanced in the direction actually played far better than if ROT or TOR
were built upon.

Let us now leave the subject of anagrams for the moment and consider two of the big awkward letters – X and J. The X and J are letters of which the best use is not usually made. Sometimes a triple-letter square will present itself so that you can score the X or J six times but not too often. AX, EX, OX, and JO can be frequently persuaded to arrange themselves on the board so as to position the X or J on a triple-letter square, scoring six times the value of the letter. The same may be done with ADZ or ZO.

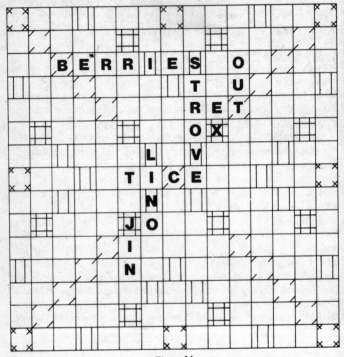

Figure 14

Your opponent has started with TICE and you have TROVENX on your rack. It would be simple to get rid of the cumbersome V by playing VEX, using the E of TICE, for a reasonable 25 points and it would also leave you with TROEN as good letters. But we wish to position an O or E in front of the triple-letter square so as to be able to place the X on it for our next move if our opponent does not use it.

WE could make NEVER or TROVE by using the E of TICE, which

would leave us with TOX and NEX respectively. Either would get rid of the V and allow the X to be scored six times by playing OX or EX should play permit. The reason for not playing EVER or ROVE is that if our opponent decides to play a word over either of these words by positioning an F, L, N or S over EVER or D, G, P or T above ROVE then such a word might spoil our intentions with whatever letter appeared two squares above the triple-letter square.

By playing NEVER we forestall this and even if TROVE has an S placed above it we are not blocked. Let's play TROVE and hope – we'll allow our opponent to place an S above it so long as he does not use the triple-letter square!

Our opponent has IOI left on his rack and these are joined by FLU? making IOIFLU?. His FOIL or FOUL are of little use to him and he could make FLOUR or FOLIO by using the R or O of TROVE but would leave himself with II? or IU? respectively. He could also create FOUL/UT/LI or FOIL/IT/LI but if he has any sense he will exchange FOILU and retain I?

So the way is clear for us and we have drawn LOIN to accompany our NEX. Let us consider LOINNEX before jumping in to score 52 points with RE/EX/OX for a seven- or eight-letter word would be better. Nothing comes to mind so we settle for 52 points.

Our opponent has got BERRS united with his I? and for simplicity we will quickly make BERRIES/STROVE.

Our LOINN has received JK, making LOINNKJ. Instead of looking for the best place (if any) for JINK or LINK let us use the I of TICE to make LINO so that the O of LINO will take the J before it on a triple-letter square and we might create JO/JINK with our next move.

The seven replacement letters received by our opponent are OUTGOAD and he simply plays OUT/RET for 12 points retaining GOAD as useful letters. Our JINK drew CEN but we do not rush to play JINK as if we merely play JO/JIN then the JIN can receive the K of NECK we are left with as a higher-scoring move next time.

* * * *

Our friendly rival has BMPRAYS and decides to play BRAYS instead of PRAYS as he prefers to retain MP and not MB, which is logically sound but wastes the S for only 26 points.

We have ROUNDEZ and, among others, our moves could be ZO/BO (25 points), BONZER or BRONZE (34 points), ADZ (33 points), or DOZY (27 points). However, if we merely place our D after the A of BRAYS, we could then have the opportunity of placing the Z on the triple-letter square with our next move so as to make ADZ/ZO or ADZ/ZONE or others. We also do not have to risk picking up an appropriate letter so as to use the Z on the triple-letter square as we already have the O or even the ERO to make ZERO. Our opponent could make a move which would block us, but he just used an S for BRAYS and only a D or S or O will go after AD. let us proceed with hope.

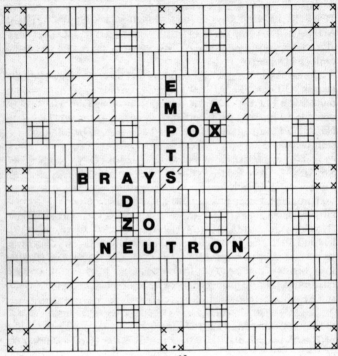

Figure 15

Our opponent now has MPTATED and being a knowledgable chap he plays EMPT before the S of BRAYS instead of making EMPTY. As EMPT is a verb (but only in Oxford) which actually means to empty he can now place his remaining T of TAD to create TEMPTS for his next move.

We pick up a T to join our ROUNEZ and after some thought we decide to form ADZ/ZO as the EN or ER or EU combinations of the TRUNE we are left with may be placed under ADZ/ZO with the E part under ADZ in a later move. So ADZ/ZO has scored 64 points with a little bit of luck.

Meanwhile TAD has received OXIL and although AXIOM or POX for 28 points look the most tempting our opponent can place the O after the P of EMPTS and hope to score the X six times in his next move. So PO it is.

TRUNE draws ON and destroys any hope we had of making TOURNEY (Oxford only) but we find that we can form NEUTRON/ADZE/OU for a phenomenal 92 points.

Our opponent, left with TADXIL, receives the K but rejoices in creating POX/AX for 53 points.

If we regard the ON of NEUTRON we may perceive it would dutifully take the JO above it while POX would accept a Y after it (POXY depends on the dictionary) and ZO will receive an S to make a six-letter word down to the bottom middle triple-word square if one uses the T of NEUTRON as the second letter of the six-letter word. One should always scan the board for obvious possibilities like this apart from the much more obvious ways of adding to AX. For example, what about S P E E D E R going beneath ADZE/OU to make ADZES/OUP/TE/RE/OD/NE/SPEEDER!

It would be a fitting remark at this point for someone to say"All this is all very well, but what do you do with EIOAIEI"? The answer is "Nothing". Or nearly nothing. If you use the AI or OE or IO you are still left with five bad letters that may be joined by two more vowels, putting you in the same position again. Here you should retain EA and exchange five letters, unless all or most of one particular vowel has appeared on the board. If the other six I's have appeared then retain AIE or IE or AI, subject to the condition of the board.

You may then observe, "But I frequently get other vowels to take their place. Sometimes this does happen, so one has to repeat the procedure till the balance is restored. This streak of misfortune is commonplace, but then it is also possible to obtain two or three seven-letter words one after the other on one's rack. C'est la vie!

Slightly different principles apply to consonants like TNNTPRD; here one must consider first what combinations of them would best contribute to a useful word or grouping of letters to be absorbed into a seven-letter word. RNT would find A or E or O most useful in either case, while DNT accepts E or I best in both alternatives. TRD would fit well with A or I or O. You notice I have avoided mention of the U because it is unwieldy. You should never think of a seven-letter word like PRINTED and exchange the T and N in the hope of making it. The odds are heavily stacked against you, and in favour of your picking up two more consonants to make you unhappier still.

With TNNTPRD one could retain RNT and exchange PNTD, unless one can use them profitably on the board, which is unlikely unless, for example, an A or E are so sited as to permit PANTED. Even then the word PANTED should not be made unless it opens up the board even further, since one would be using up good letters like NTD for little avail. The alternative here is to exchange all seven letters but it is optional according to the player and the state of play of the board.

There are some groups of letters which, although they seem at first sight to be promising, containing a fair selection of vowels and consonants, never lead to the greater things expected of them and should not be retained on your rack. Okay, 'never' becomes 'hardly ever'.

The word ORANGE springs to mind as a bad combination of letters which often occurs to tempt the player into retaining them and using or exchanging the seventh letter in the hope of making a seven-letter word. It is very rare that such an attempt will succed as only the letters C, D, R and S seem to co-operate with such an endeavour, making CORNAGE, GROANED, GROANER and ORANGERS/ONAGERS for the 50-point bonus. The letters C, D, R and S constitute only fifteen out of the other ninety-three letters apart from ORANGE (taking this as the start of the game for fairness) and your seventh letter. This means that the odds are seventy-eight to fifteen or slightly over five to one against your obtaining the necessary letter.

Odds of five to one are, as you are aware, rather formidable unless you are at the end of the game and your situation requires you to gamble for gold.

Whenever I see the letters GO sitting with others on my rack I groan a little as experience has shown that they seldom ally with others in a fruitful fashion. Naturally, if I and N sit on the rack as well then that is a different matter as OING is a constituent of many words, though usually only with another O and two consonants. If you have ORANGE, then, subject to the seventh letter, the letters G and O should be shed from your rack with indecent haste, leaving NEAR as a lovely group capable of participating in far better things.

The five-letter word DROME is another which I have toyed with in the past but found very unappealing, as it usually gets me into all sorts of trouble. I have discovered that one should get rid of the MO, subject to the other two letters on the rack, as RED is one of those popular groupings that should be utilised for greater things.

As a rule, one should discard any letter which is duplicated on one's rack, despite the number of words that contain two of the same letter. It is far safer to do this even with the letter S as it often gets one into deep water when doubled on the rack and one rarely scores a 50-point bonus using a word with two S's.

It becomes pertinent at this stage to consider the workings of some minds which lean towards the creation of possible words by using some of the letters on the rack if fitting letters can be obtained to go with them. Don't do it! Allow your letters to work themselves towards words, rather than try to make words which flirt with your hopes. The two exceptions to this rule are when you have six good letters which will accept two or three alternative letters to form a seven-letter word, or when you have four good letters and a blank.

Say you have QUETZPI. You may think of QUETZAL as being a 'darling' of a word and by strange chance you may see one or two openings where it will fit in. Forget it! Use QUIT, keeping the E to add later, or QUIP or PIQUE or ZIP or QUIZ, dependent on the condition of the board. Never use QUITE if you can usefully avoid it in a situation like this as you are wasting the E and QUITE does not lend itself easily to further use (although it is an archaic form of QUIT in Chambers).

Permit me to relax a trifle now and run through a complete game with you. With some trepidation I promise not to cheat but to allow the game to take its natural course by my left hand playing my right hand. Here goes!

Right (R) starts with AHACEXI and we can make a variety of words such as AH, AHA, EH, HE, ACHE, EACH, etc. We don't want to use the X yet as we hope to be able to quadruple its points value by later use. A little thought results in EACH (18 points) being positioned so that the double-letter square is underneath the A of EACH, ready to receive the X of EX being played underneath the A of EACH. This is hoping that Left (L) will use a B, L, P, R or T before EACH; if he does not do so then it is likely he may play so as to make a double-word square or triple-word square available for the X.

Left has received INTERIO and, unfortunately, does not see a receptive R on the board. INTER/REACH could be played for 20 points leaving H, L, N, S, T or W to be placed above INTER. HI/IO is playable for 9 points, retaining INTER (a useful group) and permitting many letters to be positioned below HI and an S or N to go after IO. We will be play for the possible greater betterment of INTER and take only 9 points with HI/IO.

R's AXI has received ZILL making AXIZILL. What a pity we don't have an E! HIE/EX/OX would have been so nice!, We could play AXIL/LEACH for 32 points or EA/AX/AX for 36 points. Either way does not leave a good grouping on the rack but either AX will acept the Z for ZAX so we will make the latter move.

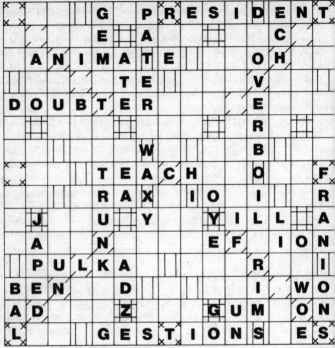

Figure 16

L's INTER is now accompanied by KU, forming INTERKU. Damn! Fortunately we can create TRUNK/TEACH/RAX for 38 points and await Lady Fortune.

R has now got IZILLAY so making ZAX will score 29 points but leave a bad cast behind on the rack. A search reveals LAZY, which won't fit usefully anywhere as I don't think TRUNKY is a word, but ILLY is an anagram of LILY or YILL and we make OY/YILL for 28 points, keeping ZAI.

L has drawn EOUSY to join IE and EOISYIE doesn't look very hopeful. To use an L of YILL to make LOUSY for 16 points is precisely that! Whatever we might play, like OKE or EKE or KIE or KY/YOU, scores little and, more importantly, leaves a bad casting on the rack. We will retain SE and exchange five letters.

R has obtained R?DO making ZAIR?DO. I cannot make a seven- or eight-letter word and can only usefully see KA/ADZ for 39 points (leaving an E to go after ADZ) or ZAX for 29 points. As I have a blank I will take the 39 points and hope to go on to better things.

L's SE get PLUIT and making UPTILES which is not really very good as I can't forge a seven- or eight-letter word at all. I could play LEAP/UP for 22 points leaving UTIES on the rack, or PULL for 10 points keeping TIES, which is much better. Then I see the word PULKA which strikes a dim chord in my memory as being the cooked fleshy leg of a chicken. It seems ridiculous to me but I play it for 22 points and then jump for the dictionary. The meaning is slightly different, 'a Lap-lander's boat-shaped sledge' but it will do as it opens the board further and I have a good group of letters in TIES. As an afterthought I could have made STIPULE or PULIEST from UPTILES but somebody else told me too late for comfort.

If you recall, R was left with ORI? which is mated with OVE causing ORI?OVE. I immediately think of OVEROIL which is what I always used to do with my cricket bat. Then comes OVERBOIL, using an L of YILL, but I cannot form any other seven- or eight-letter words. Perhaps you can? OVEROIL/ADZE will score 94 points while OVERBOIL gives only 72 points. However, somehow I cannot get rid of the feeling that OVEROIL may be hyphenated while OVERBOIL is not. I will give into my hunch and play OVERBOIL for so-called safety and dive for the dictionaries. I cannot find OVEROIL in either but OVERBOIL is in both. Lucky me! A small point – OVERBOIL is played into the first L of YILL not because it scores more than on the second L, but because it permits a seven-letter word containing an S to go after YILL.

L's TIES has been joined by CHG. Calamity! I cannot make a seven-or eight-letter word; EIGHT/ADZE scores 50 points leaving SC, ECH/ADZE totals 38 points leaving GITS, ECH/OH makes 26 points leaving GITS; if only there were a loose N I could make ETCHINGS – what a pity! As the V of OVERBOIL is not very useful I will make do with only 26 points with ECH/OH, knowing that OH will accept an O after it and if my opponent uses one triple then I can probably use the other, though the E on the top triple-line will fit in nicely with my residual GITS (GIEST ending).

R has picked up FOINW?Y. There is not much he can do except make WAXY for 21 points, retaining FOIN? as the best grouping possible.

L's GITS receives OIE, which is distinctly unhelpful, and a look around the board shows that we can only get rid of IO by using the P of PULKA or the L of YILL, POI scores 10 points, IO/PO makes 6 points but both spoil the use of the U of PULKA by the Q when available, and another U has been used up by TRUNK. IO should be used to retain GITSE as the best group of letters on the rack, so we will make LI/IO for only 4 points as IO will take an N or an S after it. Did you spot that we nearly had DIGESTION by using the D of ADZE?

R has matched FOIN? with AR and juggle as we may with FOIN?AR and the letters on the board it is very difficult to see anything other than FRANION (a loose woman). By placing FRANION/ION we score 83 points and leave an S to go after FRANION.

L kept GITSE which draws ON forming GESTION (meaning 'Conduct'), which accepts an E before it to create EGESTION, but we will search for something more beneficial. GONEIEST (top line) is not a word nor is any anagram of it. TOEINGS is not allowable as TOEING is only the present participle of the verb 'Toe' and is not substantive. It looks as if we will have to be content with GESTION/ADZE for 88 points.

R obtains TEGIRUM and twist and turn it as much as I can, I cannot create a seven- or eight-letter word. If we use MUG or GUM we will retain TIRE, which is a favourable casting of letters, and hope for well-fitting companions to join them. There are still openings on the board, especially the E on the top line and the E of OVERBOIL and the P of PULKA, although this game does not seem to be specially open or very manoeuverable. We find GUM/GO/UN for 19 points instead of MUG/MO/UN for 24 points, as GO will take letters above it while MU will not (except E) and the M of GUM will do likewhile while the G of MUG will only take a U.

L draws VEDATED which cannot find a loose I on the board for DEVIATED. We could make DUTY/EAT for 15 points, retaining EVADE, but what can we hope to select to go constructively with EVADE?Not much! DATE is a useful combination of letters but where can we put DEV? Nowhere! Let us exchange DEV.

R's TIRE has obtained WOE and rightly so! The letters TIREWOE cannot be used for a seven- or eight-letter word and it is best to use WOE and keep TIRE again. WOE/WO/ON scores 19 points, leaving ES/FRANIONS still as a possibility.

L receives JEA alongside DATE and I cannot resist JAPED for 62 points; it renders the U of PULKA unusable for the Q but it leaves us with ATE.

R obtains SDN to join TIRE which makes TINDERS but I cannot find anywhere to put it. Joyfully I include the top-line E to made RESIDENT, thinking that it will take a P before it. We look at the board and see that only one P has appeared so we make a mental reservation for the remaining P. RESIDENT scores 149 and we breathe freely again.

On L's rack appears IMPA, to be received by ATE, so we now have IMAPTEA which cannot go with the E or the R of OVERBOIL, which are the sole openings apart from underneath the R of RESIDENT. If we used PAM or MAP we would have IATE left, which is reasonable, but PAM/PRESIDENT does not allow any letter other than S to follow PAM. Two S's have appeared on the board already. If we make PRESIDENT/PA then we could use M or T to make PAM or PAT should the occasion arise. Let's do precisely that! PA/PRESIDENT scores 16 points, leaving IMTEA.

R gets FIGUREL. FIGURAL/PAL would have been wonderful, it makes one want to scream! We note that we have the last U and the Q has not yet arrived. The big question crops up – shall we retain the U or use it in a position to await the Q? Don't know! Let's survey the board. Two S's, two blanks and two D's have been played so there are two S's and two D's left to make FIGURES/PAS or FIGURED/PAD. There are 15 letters left plus L's seven letters, which makes 22 letters out of which we need any one of 4 letters. This makes 18 to 4 or 9/2 against us as the odds available. Not good! Even if FIGURER existed it would only shorten the odds to 17/5 because five R's appear on the board and our rack. We are still in the middle-game and the odds are too high. Forget it! I cannot see anything except FA/FLUE or LUGE to make life easy for the Q, and these moves will spoil PA and the E of OVERBOIL. Let us retain IER and exchange FLUG.

L's IMTEA receives AN, making ANIMATE. I cannot see anything more useful than ANIMATE/PAT; although ANIMATE/PAM would score more, the former move stretches two squares further left for future benefit, and PAT will take an E after it as well as an S. ANIMATE/PAT scores 76 points.

R's IER does not fare well with SAFE and no eight-letter word can I make with the A or N of ANIMATE nor the E or R of OVERBOIL. I would like to get rid of FE leaving myself with IRESA (RAISE) and not merely make FA/FA by using the A of PAT for 26 points. Finally I see OYE/EF/IF for an equal 26 points which is a much better move

Ugly! L has obtained QRBLDBG! There are seven letters left plus seven letters on R's rack and the last U is somewhere among them! If R uses his seven letters then L is left with the Q etc., and no letters left to take. We cannot take the chance of being caught with the Q so we will keep RD and exchange QBLBG.

The RAISE of R gets SE. How odd at this stage! The situation seems ripe merely to play an S for ES/FRANIONS for 36 points and keep EASIER.

L's RD draws ETOUT. Yes, that often occurs when one exchanges the Q! RETOUTED by using the E of OVERBOIL does not seem reasonable. TROUTED by itself might be worth a gamble but it is uninsertable. UNDERTOT is surely not a word. Wait! We returned two B's in the last exchange and one of them would help to make REDOUBT or DOUBTER. Also, the G we returned to the bag would form GROUTED. These two possibilities are both on the basis that we exchange a T. Now, R took one of the last seven letters in the bag so there must be at least two out of the three required letters left in the bag. Maybe three! The odds are at most two to one against us with the possibility of the odds being evens if R took another letter from the seven-bag-letters instead of one of the B's or the G. It seems tempting! If we place a T beneath the second A of ANIMATE then AT will receive the E of DOUBTER or GROUTED. Let's try!

EASIER obtains L making REALISE, but it will not go under AT, nor by using the A or N of ANIMATE nor the E or R of OVERBOIL can we make an eight-letter word. How frustrating! We place an E over the M of ANIMATE so that the top left triple or middle-triple word squares can be reached. We score just 4 points, keeping REALIS.

Whoopee! L got his B! Swiftly we pounce for DOUBTER/ATE for 73 points. As we reach for the last four letters our hands should freeze in mid-air. What about the Q? We deserve to get it for forgetting and putting the last U in an unusable position. No matter! 73 points should compensate for minus 10 points.

R has drawn a B to make BARLIES but it is too late – the place has gone. The only possibilities for placing a seven- or eight-letter word are to use the R of OVERBOIL or put an S after OH and end the seven-letter word with IE to be positioned before the F and R of FRANIONS. That would Mean S----IE with BARL insertable and then only if OH can be pluralised. No – let's try the ----R--- with BARLIES. Still no inspiration! Trying the N of ANIMATE and the U of DOUBTER does not give a nine-letter word; still we realise that L is stuck with his Q so we can make the best use of our letters as slowly as we like. We'll have BAL/AD/BE for 22 points retaining RISE.

L cannot get rid of the V and can only see AGON, GEN, UN/BEN so he opts for UN/BEN for 14 points.

R scores 24 with RIMS/GESTIONS.

L makes 6 with GEM.'

R finishes with PATER/TE for 9 points plus 14 points from L for the Q and the V while L subtracts 14 points from his score. The final scores are **Right 609 and Left 417**.

The best lesson to be learnt with one quick look at the board is how few double- and triple-word squares remain unused. It also seems remarkable how few triple-letter squares were used but that is just a strange chance. Although the game was fairly high-scoring it did not afford me many opportunities of putting into play the points I am trying to impart to you so we will have another try with the next game.

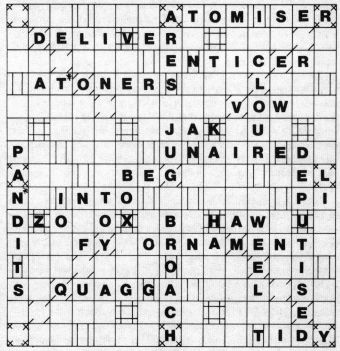

Figure 17

L commences with ETGEIEE. Do I hear cries of "That's more like it!" Yes. I'm getting the type of rack you are so frequently cursed with. Here we shall retain ETGI and exchange the others. We are keeping two vowels and two consonants but not for that reason alone; the E and the T take many letters in between them and the G and the I would be blessed with an N.

R starts with WIRMILD. Oh dear! We could place WILD or MILD on the board for 16 or 14 points leaving us with RIM or WIR respectively. But what a start! Neither WILD or MILD is receptive except for WILD taking an S after it. I would prefer, with all those letters in the bag, to retain RID and exchange the others. So be it!

ERGI has adopted BES making BEGTIES, so here we can exchange or place BEG on the board. As we have the S to go after BEG and TIES is a nice group we shall position BEG towards the left-hand side of the board and hope to make a seven-letter word from the base of TIES. I realise we could place the BEG starting from the center so as to receive the S of our hoped-for seven-letter word coming down a double-word line but remember how most games naturally gravitate towards the right.

R's RID has drawn UNEA causing RIDUNEA. It took me three minutes before I saw UNAIRED and this was after I had vainly tried to make eight-letter words using B, E or G. We can place UNAIRED so that the U is above or below the G of BEG. If above, then B, D, F, H, J, L, M, R, T and V spring to mind as letters being placeable above UG and, if below, then E, M, N, P, R T and V are placeable below GU. The E of BEG is better usable if we have UG and the RED at the end of UNAIRED makes little difference, allowing letters above or below it to reach the triple-word square. I think we'll have UG.

L's TIES has got PUE. As TIESPUE doesn't look very appetising on its own we have to try it with each of the available letters on the board in turn. I started with the B of BEG and made nothing until I reached the D of UNAIRED. How did you do? Well, DEPUTISE is better than nothing. Also, it will take an S or D after it and the alternative of DEPUTIES would be so final.

R's rack contains FLOIÇOR. I cannot make a seven- or eight-letter word with these letters, nor can I use FOCI or FICO to score 55 points by using the ISE of DEPUTISE as EC is, unhappily, not a word. I could score 26 points by using COF and the I of DEPUTISE to make COIF or 20 points with COIF and the S of DEPUTISE, but this would block the use of the S or the S and the E of DEPUTISE. As the game is so young and open I will exchange COIF and keep LOR. Yes, I know that EF/FOR/PO/UR would have scored 39 points but it would have left me with COIL.

L's rack receives JAKDINT. Here, if one can use JAK (a form of JACK) then DINT is a well-formed group for improvement. I can see 55 points with IK/KIND/SI/EN but IK is shown in the Oxford as Middle English form of I, pronoun. Though it is not marked obsolete I think its use is debatable. I can see JAK/JUG/AN/KA for 53 indisputable points, so let's have them

R's LOR has not fared very well. It has drawn UINE making LOUNIER, from which I cannot create any seven- or eight-letter word at all. If one wishes to retain NIER as a good cast of letters then LOU must be used somewhere. Let's look. If we make LOUR ('to scowl') then at least this will accept a C or F before it.

L's DINT obtains TIO. Normally TIO are favourably fitting letters but not here! I cannot make any seven- or eight-letter word out of DITTION. Obviously we want to get rid of the letters that are duplicated, but where can we put IT without spoiling a receptive area? BIT would suffice and would take an O before it and E, O, S or T after it, but I don't like being left with DINTO. The right two letters together to join DINTO would be lovely but it would be so easy to get one or two bad letters. An alternative is to make INTO/BO so that the I and N are available and BO accepts many letters after it. Also, I am left with DIT which feels more comfortable. I realise that there is only one P to go before INTO.

R's NIER has received TEC. This grouping rings a bell! ENTERIC or TERCINE or ENTICER! In any case the C will go about LOUR and the S of DEPUTISE can be used for ENTICERS. But let's not rush – perhaps there is another eight-letter word which will serve a better purpose? No, I cannot see one. ENTICER/CLOUR is a better proposition than the other two for, apart from the double-word square, it allows an S to follow ENTICER to come down from the right-hand top triple and permits a seven-letter word more room for its last one or two letters to end above or below the EN of ENTICER.

L's DIT has drawn YIEZ. Yes, I thought it was too good to last! Well, what can best be done with DITYIEZ? This is one of those situations where one has to forego thoughts of retaining letters suitable for inclusion in seven-letter words. We have the words TIDY, DIET, TIDE and DEITY, among others, but the use of the Z seems negligible. It would be useful if we could put ZIY somewhere but this seems impossible. The best solution seems TIDY/DEPUTISED for 40 points, keeping ZIE.

R has SOIFOXY. The alternatives seem clear enough, BOX/OX/TO for 55 points or EX/XI/PI for 58 points. Better to settle for 55 points and use up one of the two O's on the rack than keep two O's and use the I for just 3 points more.

ZIE receives VORL make LOVERIZ. One can score 36 points with VIZIER or VIZIR using the I of INTO or DEPUTISED respectively. In the first case one is getting rid of a bad V but the Z is not easily re-usable, nor does the position of the V enhance future moves there. The second way, with VIZIR, does permit the Z to be used quite easily but stops the S of DEPUTISED being usable. If we play ZO/IO for 33 points then one of the two remaining D's can go before it down the triple-word line. We will retain LIVER, which is not bad by itself or as a content of seven- or eight-letter words.

SOIFY on the right has drawn ME; if we get rid of FY as best we may then SOIME is a fair grouping of letters to keep in hope of better things. FY/TOY is played for 28 points.

LIVER on my left has had some luck for ED has appeared to create REVILED/DELIVER. We can choose between DELIVER/RE for 90 points, REVILED/DZO for 99 points or DELIVERS for 80 points. It must be DELIVER/RE for a loss of 9 points because RE takes A, E, G, I, O or U before it on the triple-word square and many letters after it, and the R of REVILED/DZO would need seven letters after it for a bonus while the D of DELIVER can be part of an eight-letter word and the ZO remains open for the last D.

SOIME has not prospered with LI, and it seems that the best that one can do is EL/LI/PI for 16 points. It is best not to score 31 points with MOIL/ME/ORE with the middle top triple-word square as this would waste such a beautiful opening.

SWATVLS comes to L's rack and I'm beginning to think someone has misplaced or stolen the blanks! It suffices here to place the V and W to make VOW by using the O of CLOUR as this gets rid of them nicely out of future harm's way and we keep SALTS.

R's SOIME beneficially draws TA and ATOMISE or ATOMIES springs to mind. I'm not going to spend any time looking around for anagrams or eight-letter words with the board in this condition so I plump for ATOMISE/ARE for 89 points and hope for an R, S or D to go after ATOMISE.

L's SALTS has fared badly, receiving DM and here we are presented with a dilemma but thankful that it is not a trilemma! MAD/DZO will score 31 points, MAST/FA/TOYS scores 29 points but either will leave me in a quandary by using my only vowel. As the two blanks have not appeared and I have the last two S's I think that I should retain an S and D for the openings plus A and T and exchange the S, L and M. The two S's are of little use to me as I am short of vowels and one rarely makes a seven-letter word with two S's on one's rack. Exchange.

R has QFROGEN and a quick look at the board shows that three U's have gone. We must get the Q back in the bag but what can accompany it? We perceive that FORE will fit above the DEL of DELIVER for 32 points but that will leave us with QGN which is nasty. On this side too we realise that the two blanks are probably still in the bag so we will retain REN and exchange QFOG.

L has had some luck by getting PI? to join SDAT, forming DA?PIST. What can be made of this? IST is a reasonable ending but now can PA?D be arranged before it? Going through the alphabet doesn't help. Let's go through the alphabet slowly and try each letter with the other six and the available letters on the board like the D of DELIVER and the U, T, I, S and E of DEPUTISED. Yes, the U or E can be used in an eight-letter word by careful selection of letters fitting after and before them respectively. N and S and T are useful possibilities after the U and AL, AM, AP, AS, AT, EL, EM or ES can fit before the E in many eight-letter words. I have just noticed that ARE in the top middle triple can take A, D, T, S or W after it, so let's try a seven-letter word first.

An E would make PASTIED but I don't like it as I think the right word is only PASTY. L makes PLASTID but I'm not sure if my memory is tricking me. An N would make PANDITS and I feel surer about this one though I cannot recall the meaning. An R will create DISPART of which I feel surer and I think it is an Old English word for 'separate'. I'm not going on to the eight-letter word possibilities (you may if you like) as they will not score more or improve the layout of the board except an eight-letter word ending in the E of DEPUTISED.

PANDITS/DZO will score 93 points and DISPART/ARET will score 75 points. I feel even surer of PANDITS though the meaning eludes me; my memory informs me that when I came across it in the past I instantly associated it with Pandit Nehru and Bandit. Right, PANDITS/DZO it is. I am challenged! The challenge fails but only just. Only Chambers allows PANDIT as a variant for pundit. Phew!

R's REN has obtained MOAN. The first letter of the exchange was M and I felt swindled as I had thought of FROGMEN by merely exchanging the Q but dismissed it as lunacy. Still, that sometimes happens. We now have REMOANN but I cannot make a seven-letter word so we go through the same procedure as for DAPIST?, to try to make an eight-letter word with the additional use of the S of PANDITS. I cannot make an eight-letter word from REMOANN and S, with the S of PANDITS as the first letter but perhaps you can! ODMANNER or suchlike, given by using the D of DELIVER is of no help. The U of DEPUTISED doesn't fit but the T fits beautifully for ORNAMENT while the I, S or E are of no use. ORNAMENT it is, for 70 points.

The left rack draws QHORNGS and it is by now very obvious that we must return the Q to the bag. A quick look and a count of the I's shows that nine have been played so we have no hope of an ING. Let us keep ORNS and try for the only four places left on the board for bonuses.

R has received FBROACH and counts the ten letters left in the bag. At this stage 42 points for BROACH seems reasonable, so we'll take it, using the R of ORNAMENT.

L's ORNS gets EA? and he knows he is on a winner. It is time to run through the alphabet to try to make a seven-letter word out of ORNSEA? – or an eight-letter word if you can include the H of BROACH. Do you remember that we previously tried ASTERN with many other letters? Do you recall that the inclusion of the O created SENATOR/ TREASON/ATONERS? So we have ATONERS/ARES as a starter. Let's try the only other place for a higher score, to wit, the H of BROACH. I cannot make an eight-letter word ending with H. In trying I come across CARNOSE, CORNEAS, ARENOSE, ERASION and OARSMEN. Only CORNEAS or ATONERS will do but which one will better suit the DELIV of DELIVER? It's pretty late in the game for this to assist much, but it is a useful thought for a similar position earlier in the game. We'll have ATONERS/ARES for 69 points.

On the right we now have QUAFFRG, so the Q and the U have come together at last. We realise that L has picked up the last five letters so it is imperative to use the Q now and not be caught with it. We see QUAGS, using the S of DEPUTISED, for 30 points, but that leaves us with FRG and we cannot see a loose O so that we could go out with the next move. Suddenly QUAG makes us think of QUAGGA or QUAGGY and we search for a usable A or Y. We can use the A of ORNAMENT or BROACH, for 20 or 30 points respectively, and will be left with FR which can also use either A, or the E of DELIVER and the T of ATONERS to make REFT. It is observed that ATOMISE will take the R but we will play QUAGGA and see how many letters our opponent uses.

L has WHALE but cannot use all five letters at once and R might be able to go out in one move. L can use WHAL and the E of DEPUTISED for 23 points and maybe lose 2 points if he is caught with the residual E. HAW/AD/WE at the top left scores 35 points minus 4 points for the remaining EL, if caught. If we use the A of ORNAMENT to make HA/HA/AM for 30 points we could then place LEW to make WHALE for a further 11 points by using HA if we get the chance. Also we could create HAW/WEEL for 23 points if our opponent did not finish with his next move. If we score 35 points with HAW/AD/WE minus 4 points for being caught with EL then our net worth is 31 points but if we can score HA/HA/AM for 30 points plus HAW/WEEL for 23 points then our net worth would be 53 points and the doubled value of our opponent's last letter. Let's look for the awkward letters on the board to see if our opponent is trickily placed.

The C's and V's have gone, the Q, Z, K and X are out. The B's, Y's and F's have – no, there is one F missing. So we know our opponent has an F and we can see many places for its positioning. We should work out our opponent's other letter but we feel lazy and tired and we decide to try for the highest possible score by playing HA/HA/AM for 30 points.

Using the same logic our opponent will probably know we have the W and possibly the L and may decide to play only one letter at a time if it suits him better.

R, with FR, is in a dilemma! He can score 30 points by merely playing his R for ATOMISER, less 4 points for the F if he is caught with it, which means a minimum 26 points. The F will fit nicely by the bottom right triple for EF/FY as a final 13 points. He sees that a W is missing from the board but does not proceed further with the final calculation of the letters because he is suddenly sidetracked by thinking of using the FR in one final move. He remembers REFT for 12 points and is unsure of ERF, thinking he has confused it with ERG. The 12 points from REFT will be added to by at least 6 points from his opponent's W and other two letters, and those 6 points would also be deducted from his opponent's score, making the move worth at least 24 points. But the possible 43 points from ATOMISER and EF/FY plus some from his opponent's final letters are appetising and he cannot see many places where his opponent's W and two more letters could go out in one move. He idly wishes he'd worked out the other two letters with the W and then plumps for ATOMISER for 30 points.

L is delighted and with his LEW swiftly makes HAW/WEEL for a final 23 points plus 4 points from R who must also deduct 4 points.

I cannot quite believe it! L's 550 beats R's 512. Well, Lefty got his revenge but in a goliath type of game.

This game was remarkable as I've only encountered two scores over 500 in the same game when I've played postal Scrabble. I didn't cheat but the game was played in an extremely open manner with three exchanges on each side. Once again you can see that the triple- and double-word squares have been well utilised, and that cannot be achieved with a blocked or cramped game.

Obviously, in this game we had players (if I may use that expression) who both played very openly without any qualms about the opponent's next move (until the very end) and strictly observed the open Scrabble principles. This rarely happens, more is the pity, but the extra pleasure to be derived from a game such as this should persuade more people to play openly.

7

Anagrams

Do you have trouble making anagrams? So do I, oddly enough, but the degree of trouble is lessened by practice. You may already be thinking that I am anagram-crazy but this is untrue. Seven- and eight-letter anagrams do not occupy an over-large portion of my mind in relation to other techniques of the game but they occupy a very valued place. Ordinary Scrabble® is for those who play it occasionally for fun but my type of Scrabble® is for those who are or will become zealots and, of necessity, seven- and eight-letter anagrams will become part and parcel of their everyday game.

In order to make regularly scores of 400/600 one has to develop the art of scoring the 50-point bonus so that after a time one can reasonably expect to obtain two or more such bonuses in most games. This will be allied to high-scoring abilities in other parts of the game and will soon lift you into the 400/600 range.

Often you may have a seven-letter word on your rack but not see it at all through laziness or neglect. It is essential to rearrange and shuffle your racked letters until you have exhausted all the possibilities of permutation. You must do this although at first, second or third sight you may not appear to possess a seven-letter word; MOPTORC dismayed me recently but by persistence I made COMPORT, though I then discovered I had nowhere to put it! SHUTIAN looked hopeless until I stumbled on INHAUST, thought of EXHAUST and wondered if they could possibly have opposite meanings. They had!

Your ability to make anagrams will be increased by practice, which may take many forms. Whenever you have a few moments to spare, think of an ordinary seven-letter word and rearrange the letters in different ways. Sometimes later you will perceive the same rearrangements on your rack and realise the seven-letter word you have. By engaging in this pastime on a bus or train you need no materials and are exercising that vital mental muscle. But please stop now and again to look at other people looking at you and then exercise more control over your lip movements, unless you really do not care!

When considering anagrams, it is essential to practise elongation and substitution. Elongation requires the addition of a letter to the seven-letter word so as to make an eight-letter anagram, and substitution is to replace one of the seven letters with another letter that will create another word. Here enters the most vital rule of the game, mainly associated with a blank, which is to go through the alphabet in your head and insert each letter as an alternative with the other letters on your rack and with available loose letters on the board.

Let us take the word ELATION: the addition of C makes CELATION, D forms DELATION, P gives ANTIPOLE, R makes RELATION. We did not have much success with that but let's try substituting a letter for each letter in turn.

A for E gives ALATION or AILANTO. G for E gives ANTILOG. However, in all honesty I cannot make an anagram with any of the remaining alternative letters in the alphabet. Probably you may find some and put me to shame but all I can offer by way of small consolation (to me, not you) is that if one substitutes A, B, F, G, L, O, N, R or S for the E and there is a specific usable letter on the board then we have the following:- NATIONAL, BLOATING, FLOATING, GLOATING, STALLION, NOTIONAL, NOTIONAL, RATIONAL, STALLION or SOLATION.

Now we substistute for the L of ELATION
EATION + C = ANOETIC or ACONITE   EATION + R = OTARINE
EATION + S = ATONIES   EATION + N = ENATION

Taking ELTION discover:
ELTION + I = ETIOLIN   ELTION + U = ELUTION or OUTLINE
ELTION + S = ENTOILS   ELTION + W = TOWLINE

Using ELAION I can find nothing except AILERON or ALERION or ALIENOR so we proceed to ELATON:
ELATON + B = NOTABLE   ELATON + D = TALONED
ELATON + P = NEPOTAL   ELATON + G = ANGELOT or
ELATON + S = ETALONS   TANGELO

With ELATIN we can trace:
ELATIN + A = LANIATE or ANTLIAE   ELATIN + P = PANTILE
ELATIN + E = ELATINE   ELATIN + F = INFLATE
ELATIN + G = GELATIN or ANTIGEL   ELATIN + R =
ELATIN + S = ENTAILS or SALIENT   LATRINE or ENTRAIL or
           or ELASTIN or TENAILS   RETINAL or RELIANT
                            or TRENAIL or RATLINE

ELATIO gives:
ELATIO + C = ALOETIC or COALITE
ELATIO + F = FOLIATE   ELATIO + V = VIOLATE
ELATIO + S = ISOLATE

So ELATION was reasonably successful, though not as variable as my favourite RETINAS and if you like to try the same procedure with the latter you will find the results astounding. And try adding most letters to IONATED which does not exist by itself.

If you practise elongation and substitution you will soon find that your standard of play is raised and as you train your anagrammatic muscle you will discover that it will become much stronger until it bourgeons into a reflex muscle, giving you higher scores and greater pleasure. When you get to the eight-letter word ETIOLATE and place a P in front of it making PETIOLATE, there will be no stopping you from conquering fresh fields.

Another good form of practice is to take any eight-letter word, delete the first letter and try to make another word with the remaining seven letters. Repeat this procedure with each of the letters in turn and you will be surprised at the results; for example, let us start, aptly, with CREATION.

By dropping the C we can make OTARINE, losing the R will form ANOETIC or ACONITE, excluding the E creates CAROTIN or ANTICOR. By not using the A we have CRETION or RECTION but I can't form a word by omitting the T. Dropping the I gives us ENACTOR or ORCANET. If the O is forgotten then we have CRINATE or NACRITE or CERTAIN but blocking out the N does not give me a word.

Another useful facility of this exercise is that, unknowingly, we have created seven-letter words which will all make eight-letter words by the addition of the letters we have omitted. Should we come across these words on our racks then we will know that the addition of the letters C, R, E, A, I or O will make CREATION or, if you need it, REACTION.

A more difficult exercise is once again to take CREATION and delete each letter in turn, but this time substitute another letter so as to make another eight-letter word. By dropping the C and adding D we can make RATIONED/ORDINATE/DERATION, leaving out the C and adding L we have ORIENTAL/RELATION, substituting an M for the C gives MARONITE, a P for the C gives ATROPINE, an R for the C causes ANTERIOR, finally using an S for the C creates NOTARIES/SENORITA. Losing the R only helps me to EXACTION (I hope you can do better) but cutting out the E forms FRACTION, CONTRAIL, ROMANTIC or TRACTION. The absence of the A gives CENTROID, ERECTION, CORNIEST, CONTRITE and CONTRIVE but cancelling the T gets me nowhere. The loss of the I will only show me ENACTORS/ORCANETS and then CONTRATE while deleting the O provides a plenitude in CRINATES, CENTIARE/CREATINE, CLARINET, CITRANGE/REACTING and SCANTIER. Finally we negate the N and achieve nothing.

Probably I missed some words and the more adept of you may easily put me to shame by finding them. Here are a few more suggestions of ways to oil the creaking doors of some mental departments:

1. Take any seven-letter word and divide it into two words of three and four letters. Let us take MARINES and we find MAN and SIRE, RIM and SANE, MEN and AIRS, to mention but a few. Take the E away from SIRE, making SIR and add it to MAN, forming MANE. Now we have SIR and MANE but let us make anagrams of the four-letter word, for example NAME or MEAN, so we have NAME-SIR or MEAN-SIR. Now exchange the N of NAME for the R of SIR giving RAME and SIN, and juggle RAME to cause MARE. By practising thus you will slowly provide the lubricant to the rusty or unused hinge. While doing this did the word SEMINAR appear in your mind?

2. Take some odd seven-letter words that you come across in reading-matter or elsewhere and try to make two words out of them that conjure up an odd picture in your mind; as well as the practice in making anagrams that this provides, it should help you to realise that you have a seven-letter word on your rack next time that mental picture appears. For example LARIGOT makes RIOT-GAL, and you can think of a girl starting a riot, or GOT-RAIL might cause you to picture yourself holding onto an electric rail which is such an unlikely occurrence that you should remember it as a picture. GOITRAL, an anagram, is not very far away from GOT-RAIL; just move the I between the O and T on a mental blackboard.

GLENOID is an unusual word of which I have not yet found a genuine anagram but DIE-LONG or LINE-GOD or GIN-DOLE or DINE-LOG make some interesting mental pictures. It is rather more difficult to try to remember that ELODING which does not exist but might appear on your rack is really the word GLENOID.

TEANING is not a word and seeing it on your rack would not normally cause a seven-letter word to emerge but if you make INN-GATE or NET-GAIN or NEAT-GIN then their appearance in front of you might well bring ANTIGEN or ANTEING to mind.

POTTIED does not exist until POTTY becomes a verb (if ever) but POT-DIET or TOP-TIED might create the pictures to enable you to see DIPTOTE.

IDLEMAN is an easy one because it is a word (Oxford only) and if you merely think of IDLE-MAN you are there, and the same applies to MENDOLE.

TIN-TUNE or NUT-NITE help to find INTUENT and HERE-TED or THERE-ED can cause the appropriate odd mental vision to trace ETHERED.

DIE-FIRE, as you throw water over it, will soon form REIFIED or

DEIFIER while PET-NINE may be difficult for some to visualise but PENTINE is the result and LAP-RIDE, an odd position, gives PEDRAIL (which reminds me – oddly enough, BEDRAIL is not a word). CANE-SET may trigger unpleasant memories of a headmaster but put it to TENACES, and you may even cheat with TEN-ACES.

What RED-TOES will do for some people is anybody's guess – but we get TEREDOS. SOT-DUET frequently causes a cacophony – but how about TESTUDO? RIP-TART or ART-TRIP make their own picture and lead to TRIPART. You might have difficulty in remembering TRIBADE but what about AIR-DEBT? An AIR-TENT is something many of us have experienced though TERTIAN comes to very few; NATTIER is easier (TAINTER ain't allowed) and TARTINE or ITERANT or NITRATE seem tolerable. ANTS-AIR may seem of no consequence to you but TSARINA or ARTISAN would.

I hope that by now some of you are finding it easier already to arrange letters on your mental blackboard, though other readers will not have needed this deliberate guided tour.

3. Take any two three-letter words you can think of which do not contain the letter S. Please don't use X or Z or suchlike to start with. Let us select RED HAT and juggle the letters together so we can make HATRED or THREAD and now go through the alphabet adding each letter in turn to the six letters. In order not to be prolix I will let you do it.

Now we'll have RAN and LET which will form RENTAL or ANTLER and proceed through the alphabet again. There are many seven-letter words to be made, apart from those using an S. The trick is to picture the two words on a mental blackboard if you can and allow the letters to change places until you can pounce on a word.

4. Think of four- and five-letter words that consist of reasonable vowels and consonants like ITEM or CIDER. Now switch the letters around to make EMIT, TIME or MITE and CRIED, RICED or DICER. Now go through the alphabet again and create TIMER/REMIT/MITRE and CINDER/RINCED; keep the R and try again for MINTER and CRINGED; keep those letters, try again, and you'll come up with TERMINI/INTERIM/MINTIER and DECRYING.

Now I'll give you a list of words and you can try to make anagrams from them. I shall mix the easy and the difficult and three- and four-letter words that together make a seven-letter word. The answers are on the last page.

1. TEARING	16. DUN-GORE	31. LINO-MAN	46. CAN-TRIP
2. SCEPTRE	17. RINGLET	32. ARCHING	47. RED-LOIN
3. DRAWERS	18. RUINATE	33. ERE-IOTA	48. SEATING
4. READING	19. PROTEIN	34. SIN-DOME	49. STORIES
5. MEDICAL	20. LAUNDER	35. TIN-IOTA	50. DIE-LEAN
6. LAM-ROTA	21. GENITOR	36. ERODING	51. NEITHER
7. AIR-NAME	22. INTEGER	37. FUNERAL	52. CORSETS
8. PRESENT	23. TIERING	38. LECHERY	53. SECURED
9. AILERON	24. RENTING	39. THEATRE	54. DEPOSIT
10. AILANTO	25. LATRINE	40. PELTERS	55. POSTAGE
11. FAIL-TIE	26. NATTIER	41. PLASTER	56. CUSPATE
12. REINING	27. ENTERIC	42. AIR-SEAT	57. HERNIAS
13. RODE-FUN	28. CERTAIN	43. ROT-LINE	58. TWISTED
14. RICE-TOE	29. INCITER	44. HERETIC	59. SPOILED
15. GRIEVED	30. ONE-ITCH	45. FRANTIC	60. PRAISED
			61. CALORIE

Let us digress slightly by regarding numbers, 1, 17-19, and 21-29 inclusive. They all contain the five letters INTER. There is nothing remarkable about that at first thought, but it draws to our attention the fact that INTER may be a five-letter word worthy to be aimed at for beneficial extension. I will not pretend that my efforts will be exhaustive but they should suffice to display how easy it is to make a seven-letter word by the addition of many two-letter combinations to the word INTER.

We will work alphabetically once again.

AB	+ INTER	=	ATEBRIN/RABINET
AC	+ INTER	=	CERTAIN/NACRITE/CITREAN
AD	+ INTER	=	DETRAIN/TRAINED
AE	+ INTER	=	TRAINEE/RETINAE
AF	+ INTER	=	FAINTER/FENITAR
AG	+ INTER	=	GRANITE/INGRATE/TEARING
AH	+ INTER	=	INEARTH
AI	+ INTER	=	INERTIA
AJ	+ INTER	=	JANTIER/NARTJIE
AK	+ INTER	=	KERATIN
AL	+ INTER	=	RETINAL/LATRINE/RELIANT
			TRENAIL/ENTRAIL/RATLINE
AM	+ INTER	=	MINARET/RAIMENT
AO	+ INTER	=	OTARINE
AP	+ INTER	=	PAINTER/PERTAIN/REPAINT
AR	+ INTER	=	TERRAIN/TRAINER

AS	+ INTER	=	NASTIER/RATINES/RESIANT
			RESTAIN/RETAINS/RETINAS
			RETSINA/STAINER/STARNIE
			STEARIN
AT	+ INTER	=	ITERANT/NATTIER/TERTIAN
			NITRATE/TARTINE
AW	+ INTER	=	TAWNIER/TINWARE
AU	+ INTER	=	URINATE/RUINATE
			URANITE/TAURINE
BE	+ INTER	=	BENTIER
BO	+ INTER	=	BORNITE
BT	+ INTER	=	BITTERN
BU	+ INTER	=	TRIBUNE/TURBINE
CC	+ INTER	=	CENTRIC
CE	+ INTER	=	ENTERIC/ENTICER/TERCINE
CH	+ INTER	=	CITHERN
CI	+ INTER	=	CITRINE/INCITER
			NERITIC/CRINITE
CO	+ INTER	=	CRETION/RECTION
CS	+ INTER	=	CISTERN
CT	+ INTER	=	CITTERN
DT	+ INTER	=	TRIDENT
DU	+ INTER	=	UNTRIED/UNTIRED
			TURDINE/INTRUDE
DX	+ INTER	=	DEXTRIN
DY	+ INTER	=	TINDERY
EF	+ INTER	=	FEINTER (commercial variant of
			FAINTER)
EG	+ INTER	=	TREEING/INTEGER/TEERING
EH	+ INTER	=	THEREIN/ETHERIN/NEITHER
EI	+ INTER	=	ERINITE
EK	+ INTER	=	KERNITE
EN	+ INTER	=	INTERNE
EP	+ INTER	=	PETRINE
ER	+ INTER	=	TERRINE/RENTIER/REINTER
ES	+ INTER	=	ENTRIES/TRENISE
EU	+ INTER	=	REUNITE/UTERINE/RETINUE
ET	+ INTER	=	TENTIER

FG	+ INTER	=	FERTING
FS	+ INTER	=	SNIFTER
GH	+ INTER	=	RIGHTEN
GI	+ INTER	=	TIERING/TIGRINE/IGNITER
GL	+ INTER	=	TRINGLE/TINGLER
GM	+ INTER	=	TERMING
GN	+ INTER	=	RENTING/RINGENT
GS	+ INTER	=	STINGER/RESTING
GT	+ INTER	=	RETTING/GITTERN
GW	+ INTER	=	TREWING
HI	+ INTER	=	INHERIT
HK	+ INTER	=	THINKER
HN	+ INTER	=	THINNER
HS	+ INTER	=	HINTERS
HV	+ INTER	=	THRIVEN
HW	+ INTER	=	WRITHEN
IL	+ INTER	=	NITRILE
IM	+ INTER	=	MINTIER/INTERIM/TERMINI
IN	+ INTER	=	TINNIER
IT	+ INTER	=	NITRITE
IV	+ INTER	=	INVITER/VITRINE
IW	+ INTER	=	TWINIER
JO	+ INTER	=	JOINTER
KL	+ INTER	=	TINKLER
KS	+ INTER	=	TINKERS/STINKER
KT	+ INTER	=	KNITTER/TRINKET
LO	+ INTER	=	RETINOL
LS	+ INTER	=	LINTERS/SNIRTLE
MS	+ INTER	=	MINTERS/MINSTER
NS	+ INTER	=	TINNERS/INTERNS
NV	+ INTER	=	VINTNER
OP	+ INTER	=	POINTER/PTERION/PROTEIN
			TROPINE

OS	+ INTER	=	TRIONES/TERSION/STONIER
OT	+ INTER	=	TRITONE
OU	+ INTER	=	ROUTINE
PR	+ INTER	=	PRINTER/REPRINT
PS	+ INTER	=	NIPTERS/PTERINS/TERPINS
RU	+ INTER	=	RUNTIER
SS	+ INTER	=	SINTERS/INSERTS
ST	+ INTER	=	STINTER/TINTERS
SU	+ INTER	=	UNITERS/TRIUNES
SV	+ INTER	=	STRIVEN/INVERTS
SW	+ INTER	=	WINTERS
SY	+ INTER	=	SINTERY
TU	+ INTER	=	NUTTIER
TW	+ INTER	=	TWINTER
UV	+ INTER	=	UNRIVET/VENTURI
UW	+ INTER	=	UNWRITE
UY	+ INTER	=	REUNITY

With W, V, X, Y or Z I can only see WINTERY.

Some of you may have found this expedition into the possible realms of INTER rather tedious; I found it tiring but it had two distinct purposes. Firstly, it shows you how some of the most unlikely anagrams can be made with INTER and two other letters, and secondly, it enables us to evaluate the mathematical chances of INTER.

If we count the number of two-letter additions which, when added to INTER, make one or more seven-letter words, we see that there are ninety-two. Taking into account the distribution of the letters, we can work out the chances of receiving each of those ninety-two two-letter combinations; for example, there are nine A's and twelve E's, so bearing in mind that one of the E's is already present in INTER we multiply nine by eleven and find that there are ninety-nine possible wasy of picking up AE. If this process is carried out for each of the ninety-two possible two-letter combinations and the results added together, the total is 1983.

Discounting the two blanks, there are ninety-three other letters in the game besides INTER and the arithmetical possibility of receiving any combinations of two of those letters is $\frac{93 \times 92}{1 \times 2} = 4278$ (once you have picked one of the two letters there are 92 other possible letters you could pick, so we multiply 93 by 92; because it does not matter in which order the two letters are received we divide by 2)

If we then divide the number of two-letter combinations which will make a seven-letter word with INTER by the number of possible two-letter combinations, we find that the probability of receiving the 'right' two letters is $\frac{1983}{4278} = 0.468$ i.e. the odds are about 1-1/7 to 1 – not bad! With two blanks the odds would be better than evens. If you select other likely five-letter groups such as RAISE or TRAIN you will find that similar opportunities arise. In conclusion, remember that the importance of anagrams cannot be overstressed, whether they are of three-, four-, five-, six- or seven-letter words. They serve various purposes at different times and you should practise forming them as much as you can. One does not have to be an anagrammatical genius, nor is there any need to be jealous of those people who have a natural ability for anagrams as, oddly enough, they frequently tend to be lacking in skill in other parts of the game because this ability overfeeds their egos.

To find out how well your anagrammatical muscle is developing, see if you can find the word which, when used as one or two words and inserted in the three blank spaces, will make the following sentence sensible:

The   surgeon was   to perform the operation as he had

The answer is No 61 of the anagram answers on the last page.

8
Four & Five Letter Secrets

The standard of play in Scrabble has improved by leaps and bounds in the last few years and now many players know a large part of this book before they read it. However, despite the accumulation of knowledge by many much-improved players there is always room for more. Also, it is becoming more difficult to have any 'pet' words that one is sure other people don't know. Gone are the days when one could make one or two openings on the board while feeling fairly secure that one's opponent did not know how to make use of them. Now, sometimes one's opponent knows extra letters that will fit in the openings and so confound one's ego. Come what may, I shall set out a list of words which will take a letter before or after them and then another letter after or before the product. Only those words which are open-ended both sides are worthy of inclusion and even then some are much unworthier than others.

(A)	BY	(E)	(D)	EN	(E)	(H)	OW	(E)
			(G)			(L)		
			(T)					
(F)	AIR	(Y)				(T)	ALA	(R)
(H)			(R)	AKE	(E)			
(L)								
(V)								

(B)	ALL	(Y)	(B)	ARM	(Y)	(P)	ART	(Y)
(D)						(T)		
(G)						(W)		
(P)								
(R)								
(S)								
(T)								
(W)								

(H)	AVE	(R)	(S)	CUT	(E)	(D)	EAR	(N)
(L)						(L)		
(P)						(Y)		
(R)								
(S)								
(W)								

(B) ILL (Y)
(D)
(F)
(S)
(W)

(G) LAD (Y)

(F) LAW (N)

(G) LEE (K)
(S)   (T)

(F) LIT (E)

(B) LOW (N)
(C)
(F)

(A) MEN (T)

(H) OAR (Y)
(R)

(A) LOW (E)

(R) OIL (Y)
(S)

(C) OPE (D)
(D)
(H)
(L)
(M)
(R)
(T)

(S) PAN (E)

(S) PAN (G)

(A) PER (T)

(A) RED (E)

(A) RED (D)

(B) REE (D)
(C)
(D)
(F)
(G)
(T)
(P)

(G) RID (E)

9

Eight Letter Secrets

How often do you curse when you have a bonus word which cannot be fitted on the board? Welcome to the club! However, the cursing may be reduced by paying more attention to the possibilities of using a letter on the board with your seven letters to make an eight-letter word. This is too often ignored or considered too difficult or paid too little heed by many people. Let us take the word RETAINS. Again! I may hear some of you say. Okay, why not? This is for the purpose of example, not to give you answers by rote instead of thinking, so you can similarly use the word SEATING yourself after you understand the mechanics.

Firstly, we make an alphabetical list of all letters usable with RETAINS and the eight-letter words that they make, viz.,

RETINAS

A	=	RESINATA
B	=	BANISTER/ATEBRINS
C	=	CANISTER/NACRITES/SCANTIER
D	=	STRAINED/DETRAINS
E	=	STEARINE/TRAINEES/RESINATE
F	=	FENITARS
G	=	GANISTER/GRANITES/INGRATES/ASTRINGE/
		REASTING
H	=	INEARTHS
I	=	INERTIAS/RAINIEST
K	=	KERATINS
L	=	ENTRAILS/LATRINES/TRENAILS/RATLINES
M	=	MINARETS
N	=	ENTRAINS
O	=	NOTARIES
P	=	PAINTERS/REPAINTS/PERTAINS
R	=	TRAINERS/RETRAINS/TERRAINS/RESTRAIN
S	=	STAINERS/STARNIES/RESTAINS/RETSINAS/
		STEARINS/RESIANTS
T	=	TERTIANS/NITRATES
U	=	URINATES/URANITES/RUINATES
W	=	TINWARES

It may be observed that most letters of the alphabet will combine with RETAINS and by using the formula of 93 letters of which 85, including the two blanks, will merge with RETAINS one arrives at a 91% chance of making an eight-letter word. Of course, this 91% chance will be greatly reduced by the state of the board from time to time but it is a reasonable premise to start from. Without learning the list by heart you will absorb the principle involved and only by trying it out when opportunity presents itself will you slowly begin to incorporate it as an ordinary feature of your style of play.

It is therefore useful to observe which seven-letter words reposing on the board will take another letter before or after them to sometimes make an eight-letter word. One should look as soon as the seven-letter word is deposited on the board for it is better to notice it as early as possible, so as to imprint the usable letter or letters on one's memory. This way lies the least chance of picking up a usable letter and not using it through negligence.

It is more facile to mentally pick up a usable letter from the board and place it on one's rack and then mentally shuffle it with the other letters. Do not elevate the seven letters on your rack and mingle them around a usable letter on the board, mentally of course! Do not give up after two or three mental shuffles, persevere a little longer and surprising words frequently spring to mind. Should you think this exercise too much for you then please think again. Remember the eight-letter word is multiplied by nine plus the fifty-point bonus when you use a letter reposing between two triple-word squares. Nine-timers, so to speak, are becoming more frequent occurrences in games provided that players do not rush over-hastily to use the triple-word squares through fear or greed or ignorance of better play.

If you study the words ENTRAILS/LATRINES/RATLINES/ TRENAILS you will see how easy it is to have the correct six letters and a blank as the eighth letter may repose in many places between the two triple-word squares. The word RETAINS on your rack will fit with 22 letters out of the alphabet provided the eighth letter is in the correct place or places between the two triple-word squares. It is worth learning the list by heart to enhance your chances. An oddity, but helpful is VIRTUOS. This is not a word but you know the word VIRTUOUS so knock out the second U and try to remember VIRTUOS. It takes any of the five vowels to make VIRTUOSA, VIRTUOSE, VIRTUOSI, VIRTUOSO, VIRTUOUS. It may take other letters to make other eight-letter words, but you try to find them! It will rarely appear on your rack but when it does you won't throw it away. Also by applying your mind to its construction with any of the five vowels you will discover that if any vowel is substituted for any of its letters then you merely have to find that loose letter on the board to make the same eight-letter word!

It occurred to me that it would be helpful to have a reference list of those seven-letter words (most of them) which took a letter before or after them to make an eight-letter word. I have assembled quite a formidable list at the end of the book and whilst tring to make it comprehensive I have omitted words like F,LAGGING where a letter is used three times whilst including some words like S,HOPPING which you know already.

A nine-letter word list is included with some diffidence and insouciance since to turn an eight-letter word into a nine-letter one is a rarity and I am confident that I have missed some words that are quite useful. However, for what it is worth and that ain't much I have inserted it following the eight-letter word list.

Finally, I relent, for those who had trouble with SEATING and even, in part, for those who did not I set out the near-comprehensive list at the end of the book.

10

Seven Letter Secrets

I hesitated over the inclusion of this chapter as I felt resentful at the thought of opening my pyx of treasures, which took me aeons to consider, cull and collate, for all to share. I wished to guard their existence and use them only for my selfish attempts to win more National titles. I still do! But my baser instincts have been squashed and there follows a list, in order, of the six-letter words or letter-groups most likely to acquire a seventh letter to make seven-letter words.

They are used on both Chambers and the Shorter Oxford dictionaries with a decided bias towards the Chambers dictionary because it is now used for the National Scrabble Championship. I may have missed some words along the way and you may find further anagrams that I have overlooked, but not many! Although obsolete words are not banned by the ordinary rules of Scrabble I have tended to exclude them because most Championships and Clubs do so and, as time goes by, dictionaries will also tend to drop them. This reasoning also applies to those marked 'Shakespeare, Spenser and Milton'.

The percentage figures expressed is founded on the fact of one's having seven letters on one's rack with one of them being surplus. Thus there would theoretically be ninety-three other letters available, of which some would assist and others would not. The number of those that would assist has been taken as a fraction of ninety-three and then expressed as a percentage. This is the fairest method I know as the percentage would vary according to the letters on the board and the opponent's rack at any given time.

In the list, Ch means Chambers Dictionary; Ox means the Shorter Oxford Dictionary.

1. SATIRE

A = ASTERIA (Ch only) ATRESIA
B = BAITERS BARITES
C = RACIEST STEARIC
D = ASTERID (Ch only) ASTRIDE DISRATE STAIDER
      STAIRED TIRADES
E = AERIEST SERIATE
F = FAIREST
G = AGISTER GAITERS STAGIER STRIGAE TRIAGES
                        (Ch only)
H = HASTIER SHERIAT (Ch only)
I = AIRIEST IRISATE
K = ARKITES KARITES (Ch only)
L = REALIST RETAILS SALTIER SALTIRE SLATIER
M = MAISTER MISRATE SEMITAR MASTIER
                        (Ch only)   (Ch only)
N = NASTIER RATINES RESIANT RESTAIN RETAINS
      RETINAS RETSINA STAINER STARNIE STEARIN
                                          (Ch only)
O = OTARIES
P = PARTIES PASTIER PIASTER PIASTRE PIRATES
      PRATIES (Ch only) TRAIPSE
R =   TARRIES TARSIER
S = SATIRES TIRASSE (Ch only)
T = ARTIEST ARTISTE ATTIRES STRIATE TASTIER
      TERTIAS (Ch only)
V = TAIVERS VASTIER
W = WAISTER WAITERS WARIEST

2.   MASTER

A = RETAMAS (Ch only)
B = TAMBERS (Ch only)
C = MERCATS (Ch only)
D = SMARTED
E = STEAMER   TEAMERS   (Ch only)
H = HAMSTER
I = MAISTER   MISRATE   MASTIER   SEMITAR
                        (Ch only)   (Ch only)

K = MARKETS
L = ARMLETS   MARTELS   MARLEST
M = STAMMER
N = MARTENS   SMARTEN   SARMENT
O = AMORETS   (Ch only)   MAESTRO   (Ch only)
P = STAMPER   TAMPERS
R = SMARTER
S = MASTERS   STREAMS
T = MATTERS   SMATTER
U = MATURES   STRUMAE   (Ch only)
W = WARMEST
Y = MASTERY

N.B. This one takes all the vowels

102

3.   BREAST

A	=	ABATERS	(Ox only)	ABREAST	
B	=	BARBETS		STABBER	RABBETS
D	=	DABSTER			
B	=	BEATERS		BERATES	REBATES
G	=	BARGEST	(Ch only)		
H	=	BATHERS		BREATHS	
I	=	BAITERS		BARITES	
L	=	BLASTER		STABLER	
M	=	TAMBERS	(Ch only)		
N	=	BANTERS			
O	=	BOASTER		BOATERS	
R	=	BARTERS			
S	=	BASTERS		BREASTS	
T	=	BATTERS			
U	=	ARBUTES			
V	=	BRAVEST			
W	=	BRAWEST		WABSTER	(Ch only)
X	=	BAXTERS	(Ox only)		
Y	=	BETRAYS			

N.B. This one takes all the vowels

4.   DINETS

A	=	DETAINS	INSTEAD	SAINTED	STAINED
B	=	BIDENTS			
D	=	DISTEND			
E	=	DESTINE			
F	=	SNIFTED			
G	=	STINGED			
I	=	INDITES			
K	=	KINDEST			
L	=	DENTILS			
N	=	INDENTS	INTENDS		
O	=	DITONES			
P	=	STIPEND			
R	=	TINDERS			
S	=	DISNEST	DISSENT	SNIDEST	
T	=	STINTED			
U	=	DISTUNE	DUNITES	(Ch only)	
Y	=	DENSITY	DESTINY		

N.B. This takes all the vowels, too!

5. STORED

A	= DOATERS	ROASTED	TORSADE (Ch only)	
B	= DEBTORS			
E	= OERSTED	ROSETED (Ch only)	TEREDOS (Ox only)	
F	= DEFROST	FROSTED		
G	= STODGER			
H	= SHORTED			
I	= EDITORS	ROISTED	SORTIED (Ch only)	
	STEROID (Ch only)		STORIED	TRIODES
K	= STROKED			
L	= OLDSTER	STRODLE (Ch only)		
M	= STORMED			
N	= RODENTS	SNORTED		
O	= ROOSTED			
P	= DEPORTS	SPORTED		
R	= DORTERS			
T	= DOTTERS (Ox only)			
U	= DETOURS	DOUTERS (Ch only)	OUTREDS (Ch only)	ROUSTED
W	= STROWED	WORSTED		
Y	= DESTROY	STROYED (Ox only)		

N.B. Takes all the vowels.

6. DENSER

A = DEANERS   DENARES   ENDEARS
    (Ch only)   (Ox only)
B = BENDERS
C = DECERNS
D = REDDENS
E = SNEERED
F = FENDERS
G = GENDERS
H = HERDENS   (Ch only)
I = DENIERS
L = LENDERS   SLENDER
M = MENDERS
O = ENDORSE
P = SPENDER
R = RENDERS
S = REDNESS   SENDERS
T = STERNED   TENDERS
U = ENDURES   ENSURED
V = VENDERS

N.B. This one takes all the vowes

7. TUNERS

A = AUNTERS   (Ch only)   NATURES   SAUNTER
B = BURNETS
C = ENCRUST
D = RETUNDS
E = NEUTERS   TENURES
G = GUNTERS   GURNETS
H = HUNTERS   SHUNTER
I = TRIUNES   UNITERS
K = TUNKERS   (Ch only)
L = RUNLETS
M = STERNUM
N = RUNNETS   (Ch only)   STUNNER
O = TONSURE
P = PUNSTER   PUNTERS
R = RETURNS   TURNERS
S = UNRESTS
T = ENTRUST   NUTTERS

8.   RETINA

B	=	ATEBRIN	(Ch only)	RABINET	(Ox only)
C	=	CERTAIN	CITREAN	CRINATE	
		NACRITE	(Ch only)	CANTIER	(Ch only)
D	=	DETRAIN	TRAINED		
E	=	RETINAE	TRAINEE		
F	=	FAINTER			
G	=	GRANITE	INGRATE	TEARING	
H	=	INEARTH			
I	=	INERTIA			
J	=	JANTIER			
K	=	KERATIN			
L	=	ENTRAIL	LATRINE	RATLINE	RELIANT
		RETINAL	TRENAIL		
M	=	MINARET	RAIMENT		
N	=	ENTRAIN			
O	=	OTARINE	(Ch only)		
P	=	PAINTER	PERTAIN	REPAINT	
R	=	RETRAIN	TERRAIN	TRAINER	
S	=	NASTIER	RATINES	RESIANT	RESTAIN
		RETAINS	RETINAS	RETSINA	STAINER
		STARNIE	(Ch only: see STERN)	STEARIN	
T	=	NATTIER	NITRATE	TERTIAN	TARTINE
U	=	RUINATE	TAURINE	URANITE	URINATE
W	=	TAWNIER	TINWARE		

9. ASTERN

B	=	BANTERS		
C	=	CANTERS	CARNETS	NECTARS	RECANTS
		TANRECS	(Ch only)		TRANCES
D	=	STANDER	STERNAD	(Ox only)	
E	=	EARNEST	EASTERN	NEAREST	RATEENS
					(Ch only)
G	=	ARGENTS	GARNETS	STRANGE	
H	=	ANTHERS	THENARS		
I	=	NASTIER	RATINES	RESIANT	RESTAIN
		RETAINS	RETINAS	RETSINA	STAINER
		STARNIE (Ch only: see STERN)	STEARIN		
K	=	RANKEST	STARKEN	TANKERS	
L	=	ALTERNS	ANTLERS	RENTALS	SALTER
		STERNAL			
M	=	MARTENS	SMARTEN	SARMENT	
N	=	TANNERS			
O	=	ATONERS	SENATOR	TREASON	
P	=	ARPENTS	(Ch only)	ENTRAPS	PANTERS
		PARENTS	PASTERN	TREPANS	
R	=	ERRANTS	RANTERS		
S	=	SARSNET	(Ch only)	TRANSES	(Ch only)
T	=	NATTERS	RATTENS		
U	=	AUNTERS	(Ch only)	NATURES	SAUNTER
V	=	SERVANT	TAVERNS	VERSANT	
W	=	WANTERS			

10.   LITRES

83% chance using Chambers
81% chance using Oxford

A	= REALIST	RETAILS	SALTIER	SALTIRE
	SLATIER			
B	= BLISTER	BRISTLE		
C	= RELICTS			
E	= LEISTER	STERILE		
F	= FILTERS	TRIFLER	TRIFLES	
G	= GLISTER	GRISTLE		
H	= SLITHER			
I	= SILTIER			
K	= KILTERS			
L	= STILLER	TILLERS	TRELLIS	
M	= MILTERS			
N	= LINTERS	SNIRTLE		
O	= LOITERS	TOILERS		
P	= SPIRTLE	TRIPLES		
S	= LISTERS			
T	= LITTERS	TILTERS	TITLERS	
U	= RULIEST	(Ch only)	LUSTIER	
Y	= RESTILY	(Ch only)		

N.B. This takes all the vowels

108

11. TASTER

```
B  =  BATTERS
C  =  CATTERS    (Ch only)      SCATTER
D  =  STARTED
E  =  ESTREAT    RESTATE
G  =  TARGETS
H  =  HATTERS    SHATTER        THREATS
I  =  ARTIEST    ARTISTE        ATTIRES      STRIATE
      TASTIER    TERTIAS        (Ch only)
L  =  RATTLES    SLATTER        STARTLE
M  =  MATTERS    SMATTER
N  =  NATTERS    RATTENS
O  =  ROTATES    TOASTER
P  =  PATTERS    SPATTER        TAPSTER
R  =  RATTERS    RESTART        STARTER
S  =  STATERS    TASTERS
T  =  TATTERS
U  =  STATURE
W  =  SWATTER    (Ch only)      TEWARTS      (Ch only)
Y  =  YATTERS    (Ch only)
```

12. LATENS

A	= SEALANT	(Ch only)		
C	= CANTLES	LANCETS	SCANTLE	
D	= SLANTED			
E	= ELANETS	LEANEST		
G	= LANGEST	TANGLES		
H	= HANTLES			
I	= ELASTIN	ENTAILS	SALIENT	
	STANIEL	(Ch only)	TENAILS	(Ch only)
K	= ANKLETS			
M	= MANTELS	MANTLES	LAMENTS	
N	= STANNEL	(Ch only)		
O	= ETALONS	(Ch only)		
P	= PLATENS			
R	= ALTERNS	ANTLERS	RENTALS	SALTERN
	STERNAL			
T	= LATTENS	TALENTS		
U	= ELUANTS	(Ch only)	UNSLATE	
V	= LEVANTS			
Y	= STANYEL	(Ch only)		
Z	= ZELANTS	(Ch only)		

N.B. This takes all the vowels

3
4
2

13.   EASTER

82% chance using Chambers
78% chance using Oxford

A = AERATES
B = BEATERS   BERATES   REBATES
C = CREATES   SECRETA   (Ch only)
D = DEAREST   DERATES   REASTED   (Ch only)
F = FEASTER
G = ERGATES   (Ch only)
H = HEATERS   REHEATS   THEREAS
I = AERIEST   SERIATE
K = SAKERET
L = ELATERS   RELATES   STEALER   EARLETS
                                                (Ox only)
M = STEAMER   TEAMERS   (Ch only)
N = EARNEST   EASTERN   NEAREST   RATEENS
                                                (Ch only)
O = ROSEATE
P = REPEATS   SPERATE   (Ox only)
R = SERRATE   TEARERS
S = SAETERS   (Ch only)   SEATERS
T = ESTREAT   RESTATE
U = AUSTERE
W = SWEATER

14. GRAINS

A	=	NAGARIS	SANGRIA	SARANGI	
		(Ch only)	(Ch only)	(Ch only)	
B	=	BARINGS	(Ox only)		
C	=	SACRING	SCARING		
D	=	DARINGS			
E	=	ERASING	GAINERS	REGAINS	
		REGINAS	SEARING	SERINGA	
		(Ch only)		(Ch only)	
F	=	FARINGS	FARSING	(Ch only)	
I	=	RAISING	SAIRING	(Ch only)	
K	=	RAKINGS	(Ch only)	SARKING	
M	=	ARMINGS	MARGINS		
N	=	SNARING			
O	=	ORIGANS	SOARING	IGNAROS	SIGNORA
		(Ox only)		(Ch only)	(Ch only)
P	=	PARINGS	(Ox only)	SPARING	
R	=	SARRING	(Ch only)		
T	=	RATINGS	STARING		
V	=	RAVINGS			
W	=	RAWINGS	(Ch only)		(see ROWEN)
Y	=	SIGNARY	(Ch only)	SYRINGA	

15.   SILENT

81% chance using Chambers
78% chance using Oxford

A	=	ELASTIN	ENTAILS	SALIENT	
		STANIEL	(Ch only)	TENAILS	(Ch only)
C	=	CLIENTS	STENCIL		
D	=	DENTILS			
E	=	TENSILE			
G	=	SINGLET	TINGLES		
I	=	INLIEST	LINTIES		
K	=	TINKLES			
L	=	LENTILS	LINTELS		
N	=	LINNETS			
O	=	ENTOILS			
P	=	PINTLES			
R	=	LINTERS	SNIRTLE		
S	=	ENLISTS	LISTENS	TINSELS	
U	=	LUTEINS	UNTILES	UTENSIL	
V	=	VENTILS			
W	=	WINTLES	(Ch only)		

N.B. This one takes all the vowels

16.   DINERS

81% chance using Oxford
76% chance using Chambers

A	=	RANDIES	(Ch only)	SANDIER	SARDINE
B	=	BINDERS		REBINDS	
C	=	CINDERS		DISCERN	
E	=	DENIERS		NEREIDS	
F	=	FINDERS		FRIENDS	
G	=	DINGERS	(Ch only)	ENGIRDS	
H	=	HINDERS		SHRINED	
I	=	INSIDER			
K	=	REDSKIN			
L	=	RINDLES	(Ox only)		
M	=	MINDERS		REMINDS	
N	=	DINNERS			
O	=	INDORSE		ROSINED	SORDINE
P	=	PINDERS			
T	=	TINDERS			
U	=	INSURED			
W	=	REWINDS		WINDERS	

N.B. This takes all the vowels

113

17.   INSERT

80% chance using Chambers
74% chance using Oxford

A	=	NASTIER	RATINES	RESIANT	RESTAIN
		RETAINS	RETINAS	RETSINA	STAINER
		STARNIE	(Ch only:	see STERN)	STEARIN
C	=	CISTERN	CRETINS		
D	=	TINDERS			
E	=	ENTIRES	ENTRIES	TRENISE	NERITES
				(Ch only)	
F	=	SNIFTER			
G	=	RESTING	STINGER		
H	=	HINTERS	(Ox only)		
K	=	STINKER	TINKERS		
L	=	SNIRTLE	(Ch only)	LINTERS	
M	=	MINSTER	MINTERS		
N	=	TINNERS			
O	=	ORIENTS	NORITES	STONIER	TERSION
			(Ch only)		(Ch only)
P	=	NIPTERS	PTERINS	TERPINS	
		(Ch only)	(Ch only)	(Ox only)	
S	=	INSERTS	SINTERS		
T	=	STINTER	TINTERS	(Ch only)	
U	=	TRIUNES	UNITERS		
V	=	INVERTS			
W	=	TWINERS	WINTERS		
Y	=	SINTERY	(Ch only)		

18.   RESENT

80% chance using Chambers
78% chance using Oxford

A	=	EARNEST	EASTERN	NEAREST	RATEENS (Ch only)
C	=	CENTRES			
D	=	TENDERS	STERNED		
E	=	ENTREES	RETENES		
G	=	GERENTS	REGENTS		
I	=	ENTIRES	ENTRIES	TRENISE (Ch only)	NERITES (Ch only)
L	=	RELENTS			
N	=	TENNERS			
P	=	PRESENT	REPENTS	SERPENT	
R	=	RENTERS	STERNER		
S	=	RESENTS	STRENES		
T	=	TENTERS	TESTERN		
U	=	NEUTERS	TENURES		
V	=	VENTERS			
W	=	WESTERN			
X	=	EXTERNS			
Y	=	STYRENE (Ch only)		YESTERN (Ch only)	

19.   SATINE

B	=	BESAINT	BESTAIN	
C	=	CANIEST	CINEAST (Ch only)	
D	=	DETAINS	INSTEAD	SAINTED	STAINED
E	=	ETESIAN		
F	=	FAINEST	NAIFEST	
G	=	EASTING	EATINGS	INGATES
		INGESTA	SEATING	SIGNATE	TANGIES
		(Ch only)		(Ox only)	(Ch only)
		TEASING	TSIGANE (Ch only)	
I	=	ISATINE		
J	=	JANTIES		
K	=	INTAKES		
L	=	ELASTIN	ENTAILS	SALIENT
		STANIEL	(Ch only)	TENAILS	(Ch only)
M	=	ESTAMIN	INMATES	MAINEST	MANTIES
		(Ox only)			(Ch only)
		TAMINES	(Ch only)	
O	=	ATONIES		
P	=	PANTIES	SAPIENT	SPINATE (Ch only)
R	=	NASTIER	RATINES	RESIANT	RESTAIN
		RETAINS	RETINAS	RETSINA	STAINER
		STARNIE	(Ch only: | see STERN)	STEARIN
S	=	ENTASIS	SESTINA	TANSIES	TISANES
			(Ch only)		(Ch only)
T	=	INSTATE	SATINET	
U	=	AUNTIES	SINUATE	
V	=	NATIVES	NAIVEST	VAINEST
W	=	WANTIES	(Ch only)	TAWNIES	(Ch only)
X	=	TAXINES	(Ox only)	
Z	=	ZANIEST		

20. RAISED

B	=	BRAISED	DARBIES	
C	=	RADICES	SIDECAR (Ch only)	
E	=	DEARIES	READIES	
F	=	FRAISED		
G	=	AGRISED (Ch only)		
H	=	DEARISH	SHADIER	
I	=	DAIRIES	DIARIES	
K	=	DAIKERS (Ch only)		
L	=	DERAILS	SIDERAL	
M	=	ADMIRES	MISREAD	SIDEARM
N	=	RANDIES (Ch only)	SANDIER	SARDINE
O	=	SOREDIA		
P	=	ASPIRED	DESPAIR	DIAPERS	PRAISED
R	=	RAIDERS		
T	=	ASTERID (Ch only)	ASTRIDE	DISTRATE
		STAIDER	STAIRED	TIRADES
U	=	RESIDUA		
V	=	ADVISER	VARDIES (Ch only)	
X	=	RADIXES		
Z	=	AGRIZED (Ch only)		

21. SATING

A = AGAINST
B = BASTING
C = ACTINGS   CASTING
D = EASTING   EATINGS   INGATES
    INGESTA   SEATING   SIGNATE   TEASING
    (Ch only)   (Ox only)
    TSIGANE   (Ch only) TANGIES (Ch only)
F = FASTING
G = STAGING
H = HASTING   TASHING   (Ch only)
K = SKATING   STAKING   TAKINGS
L = LASTING   SALTING   SLATING
M = MASTING   MATINGS   TAMINGS
N = ANTINGS   (Ch only)
O = AGONIST   (Ch only)
P = PASTING   TAPINGS
R = RATINGS   STARING
T = STATING   TASTING
V = STAVING
W = WASTING   STAWING
X = TAXINGS
Y = STAYING

22.   HEARTS

B	=	BATHERS	BREATHS	
C	=	CHASTER	RATCHES	
D	=	DEARTHS	HARDEST	HATREDS	THREADS
		TRASHED		
E	=	HEATERS	REHEATS	THEREAS
F	=	FATHERS	SHAFTER	(Ch only)
G	=	GATHERS		
H	=	HEARTHS		
I	=	HASTIER	SHERIAT	(Ch only)
L	=	HALTERS	HARSLET	LATHERS
		SLATHER	(Ch only)	THALERS	(Ch only)
M	=	HAMSTER		
N	=	ANTHERS	THENARS	
O	=	EARSHOT		
P	=	SPARTHE	TERAPHS	THREAPS
		(Ch only)	(Ox only)	
S	=	RASHEST	SHASTER	
T	=	HATTERS	SHATTER	THREATS
V	=	HARVEST	THRAVES	
W	=	THAWERS	(Ch only)	WREATHS

23.   SARDEL

C	=	SCALDER	(Ch only)	
D	=	LADDERS	RADDLES	
E	=	DEALERS	LEADERS	
F	=	FARDELS		
G	=	DARGLES	(Ch only)	
H	=	HERALDS		
I	=	DERAILS	SIDERAL	
K	=	DARKLES		
M	=	MEDLARS		
N	=	DARNELS	LANDERS	SLANDER
O	=	LOADERS	RELOADS	
P	=	PEDLARS		
R	=	LARDERS		
S	=	SARDELS	(Ch only)	
T	=	DARTLES		
U	=	LAUDERS		
Z	=	DARZELS		

24.   LADIES

B	=	DISABLE		
D	=	LADDIES		
E	=	AEDILES	DEISEAL	(Ch only)
F	=	DISLEAF		
I	=	DAILIES	LIAISED	SEDILIA (Ch only)
L	=	DALLIES	SALLIED	
M	=	MISDEAL	MISLEAD	
N	=	DENIALS	SNAILED	
O	=	DEASOIL	(Ch only)	
P	=	ALIPEDS	PALSIED	PAIDLES (Ch only)
R	=	DERAILS	SIDERAL	
S	=	AIDLESS	DEASILS	(Ch only)
T	=	DETAILS	DILATES	
U	=	DEASIUL	(Ch only)	
V	=	DEVISAL		
Y	=	DIALYSE	EYLIADS	(Ch only)

25.   SAILER

A	=	AERIALS			
B	=	BAILERS			
C	=	ECLAIRS	(Ch only)	SCALIER	CLARIES
D	=	DERAILS	SIDERAL		
E	=	REALISE			
F	=	FERIALS	(Ch only)		
H	=	SHALIER			
I	=	SAILIER	(Ch only)		
J	=	JAILERS			
K	=	SERKALI			
L	=	RALLIES			
M	=	MAILERS	(Ch only)	REALISM	
N	=	ALINERS	LAINERS	NAILERS	
		(Ox only)	(Ox only)		
P	=	PARLIES	(Ch only)	(see: Parliament)	
R	=	RAILIERS	RERAILS		
S	=	AIRLESS	SAILERS	SERIALS	
T	=	REALIST	RETAILS	SALTIER	SALTIRE
		SLATIER			
W	=	WAILERS			

26. SINGER

A = ERASING   GAINERS   REGAINS   SEARING
    SERINGA   (Ch only)
C = CRINGES   SCRINGE
E = GREISEN
F = FINGERS   FRINGES
G = GINGERS   NIGGERS   SNIGGER
L = GIRNELS   (Ch only)   LINGERS   SLINGER
M = GERMINS   (Ch only)   MEGRINS   (Ox only)
N = ENRINGS
O = ERINGOS   REGIONS   SIGNORE   (Ch only)
P = SPRINGE   PINGERS   (Ch only)
R = RINGERS   SERRING
S = INGRESS   RESIGNS   SINGERS
T = RESTING   STINGER
U = REUSING   RUEINGS
V = SERVING   VERSING
W = SWINGER   WINGERS

27. ALTERS

B	= BLASTER	STABLER		
C	= CARTELS	TARCELS	(Ch only)	
D	= DARTLES			
E	= EARLETS	(Ox only)	ELATERS	REALEST
	RELATES	STEALER		
F	= FALTERS			
G	= LARGEST			
H	= HALTERS	HARSLET	LATHERS	
	SLATHER	(Ch only)	THALERS	(Ch only)
I	= REALIST	RETAILS	SALTIER	SALTIRE
	SLATIER			
K	= TALKERS	STALKER		
L	= STALLER	(Ox only)	TELLARS	STELLAR
M	= ARMLETS	MARLEST	MARTELS	
N	= ALTERNS	ANTLERS	RENTALS	SALTERN
	STERNAL			
O	= OESTRAL	(Ch only)		
P	= PALTERS	PERSALT	(Ox only)	PLASTER
	PLATERS	PSALTER	STAPLER	
S	= LASTERS	SALTERS	SLATERS	TARSELS (Ch only)
T	= RATTLES	SLATTER	STARTLE	TATLERS (Ch only)
V	= VARLETS	VESTRAL	(Ch only)	
W	= WASTREL			
Y	= STEARYL	(Ox only)		

```
C  =  CARTING     CRATING     TRACING
D  =  DARTING     TRADING
E  =  GRANITE     INGRATE     TEARING
F  =  FARTING     RAFTING
G  =  GRATING
I  =  AIRTING     RAITING
K  =  KARTING     (Ch only)
L  =  RATLING
G  =  MIGRANT
N  =  RANTING
O  =  ORATING
P  =  PARTING     PRATING     TRAPING     (Ch only)
R  =  TARRING
S  =  RATINGS     STARING
T  =  RATTING     TARTING
Y  =  GIANTRY
```

29. TORIES

A	= OARIEST	OTARIES		
B	= ORBIEST			
C	= TERCIOS			
D	= EDITORS	ROISTED		
	ROSITED	SORTIED	STEROID	STORIED
	(Ch only)	(Ch only)	(Ch only)	
F	= FOISTER	(Ch only)	FORTIES	
G	= GOITRES	GORIEST		
H	= HERIOTS	HORIEST	(Ox only)	
K	= ROKIEST			
L	= LOITERS	TOILERS		
M	= EROTISM	MOISTER		
N	= ORIENTS	STONIER	TERSION	TRIONES
			(Ch only)	(Ch only)
O	= SOOTIER	TOORIES	(Ch only)	
P	= PORIEST	REPOSIT	RIPOSTE	ROPIEST
	(Ch only)			
R	= ROISTER	RORIEST	(Ch only)	
S	= SORTIES	TOSSIER	(Ch only)	
T	= STOITER	(Ch only)		
U	= OURIEST	(Ch only)		
V	= TORSIVE	(Ch only)		
W	= OWRIEST	(Ch only)		

30. UNDERS

74% chance using Chambers
78% chance using Oxford

A = ASUNDER
B = BURDENS
D = DUNDERS
E = ENDURES   ENSURED
F = REFUNDS
G = GERUNDS
H = HURDENS
I = INSURED
L = RUNDLES
N = DUNNERS   (Ox only)
O = RESOUND   SOUNDER
P = SPURNED
S = SUNDERS   UNDRESS
T = DUNTERS   (Ox only)   RETUNDS
U = UNSURED   (Ch only)
Y = DUNSERY   (Ox only: see DUNCE)

31. OTHERS

74% chance using Chambers
69% chance using Oxford

A = EARSHOT
B = BOTHERS
C = ROTCHES   TORCHES
D = SHORTED
F = FOTHERS
I = HERIOTS   HORIEST   (Ox only)
L = HOLSTER
M = MOTHERS   SMOTHER
N = SHORTEN
O = HOOTERS   SHOOTER
P = POTHERS   STROPHE
R = SHORTER
S = TOSHERS
T = HOTTERS   (Ch only)
U = SHOUTER
X = EXHORTS

32. PRIEST

74% chance using Chambers or Oxford

A	=	PARTIES	PASTIER	PIASTER	PIASTRE
		PIRATES	TRAIPSE		
E	=	SPIRTED	STRIPED		
E	=	RESPITE			
H	=	HIPSTER			
I	=	TIPSIER			
L	=	SPIRTLE	TRIPLES		
M	=	IMPREST	(Ch only)	PERMITS	PRIMEST
N	=	NIPTERS	PTERINS	TERPINS	
		(Ch only)	(Ch only)	(Ox only)	
O	=	PORIEST	REPOSIT	RIPOSTE	ROPIEST
		(Ch only)			
P	=	TIPPERS			
S	=	ESPRITS	PRIESTS	SPRITES	STIRPES
		STRIPES			
T	=	SPITTER	TIPSTER		
X	=	EXTIRPS			
Y	=	PYRITES			

33. SITTER

73% chance using Chambers
63% chance using Oxford

A	=	ARTIEST	ARTISTE	ATTIRES	STRIATE
		TASTIER			
B	=	BITTERS			
C	=	TRISECT			
E	=	TESTIER			
F	=	FITTERS	TITFERS	(Ch only)	
H	=	HITTERS			
J	=	JITTERS			
K	=	SKITTER	(Ch only)		
L	=	LITTERS	SLITTER		
N	=	STINTER	TINTERS		
O	=	STOITER	(Ch only)		
P	=	PITTERS	SPITTER		
R	=	RITTERS			
S	=	SITTERS			
T	=	TITTERS			
V	=	TRIVETS			
W	=	TWISTER			

34.   THRICE

72% chance using Chambers
57% chance using Oxford

A = THERIAC   (Ch only)
D = DITCHER
E = ETHERIC   HERETIC
I = ITCHIER
K = THICKER
M = THERMIC
N = CITHERN
O = ROTCHIE   THEORIC
P = PITCHER
R = RICHTER   (Ch only)
S = CITHERS   RICHEST
T = CHITTER

35.   MISTER

72% chance using Chambers
.54% chance using Oxford

A = MAISTER   MISRATE   MAESTRI ?
     SEMITAR   (Ch only) MASTIER   (Ch only)
C = METRICS   CRETISM
E = METIERS   TREMIES   TRISEME
     (Ch only) (Ch only) (Ch only)
E = FREMITS   (Ch only)
H = HERMITS   SMITHER
I = MIRIEST
L = MILTERS
N = MINTERS
O = EROTISM   MOISTER
P = IMPREST   (Ch only)   PERMITS   PRIMEST
S = MISTERS   SMITERS   (Ch only)
T = METRIST
U = MUSTIER
Y = MISTERY   SMYTRIE   (Ch only)
          N.B. This one takes all the vowels

36.   SNIPER

72% chance using Chambers
50% chance using Oxford

A	=	PANSIER	(Ch only)	RAPINES
C	=	PINCERS		
D	=	PINDERS		
E	=	REPINED		
G	=	PINGERS	(Ch only)	SPRINGE
I	=	PIRNIES	(Ch only)	SNIPIER SPINIER
K	=	PERKINS	(Ch only)	(see PARKIN)
N	=	PINNERS	SPINNER	
O	=	ORPINES	PIONERS	(Ch only)
P	=	NIPPERS	SNIPPER	
S	=	SNIPERS		
T	=	NIPTERS	PTERINS	TERPINS
		(Ch only)	(Ch only)	(Ox only)
U	=	PURINES		

N.B. Takes all the vowels

37.   DARING

72% chance using Chambers
66% chance using Oxford

B	=	BARDING	(Ch only)	BRIGAND	
C	=	CARDING			
E	=	AREDING	EARDING	GRADINE	GRAINED
			(Ch only)		
F	=	FARDING	(Ch only)		
G	=	GRADING		NIGGARD	
I	=	RAIDING			
K	=	DARKING	(Ox only)		
L	=	DARLING		LARDING	
N	=	DARNING			
O	=	ADORING	GRADINO	(Ch only)	ROADING
		IDORGAN			
P	=	DRAPING			
S	=	DARINGS			
T	=	DARTING			
U	=	DAURING	(Ch only)		
W	=	WARDING		DRAWING	
Y	=	YARDING			

38. SANDER

B	=	BANDERS		
C	=	DANCERS		
D	=	DANDERS		
E	=	DEANERS	DENARES	ENDEARS
		(Ch only)	(Ox only)	
F	=	FARDENS	(Ch only)	
G	=	DANGERS	GANDERS	GARDENS
H	=	HANDERS		
I	=	RANDIES	(Ch only)	SANDIER	SARDINE
K	=	DARKENS		
L	=	DARNELS	LANDERS	SLANDER
M	=	REMANDS		
P	=	PANDERS		
R	=	DARNERS	ERRANDS	
S	=	SANDERS	SARSDEN	(Ch only)
T	=	STANDER	STERNAD	(Ox only)
U	=	ASUNDER		
W	=	DAWNERS	(Ch only)	WANDERS
	=	ZANDERS	(Ch only)	

39.   TONERS

A = ATONERS   SENATOR   TREASON
C = CONSTER   (Ch only)   CORNETS
D = RODENTS   SNORTED
G = GRONTES   (Ox only)
H = HORNETS   THRONES
O = ORIENTS   STONIER   TERSION   TRIONES
              (Ch only)   (Ch only)

K = STONKER   (Ch only)
L = LENTORS
M = MENTORS   MONSTER   MORNEST   (Ch only)
N = STONERN   (Ch only)
O = ENROOTS
P = PRONEST   POSTERN
R = SNORTER
S = STONERS
T = SNOTTER   STENTOR
U = TONSURE

40.   CATERS

D = REDACTS
E = CREATES   SECRETA   (Ch only)
H = CHASTER   RATCHES   ARCHEST
I = RACIEST   STEARIC
K = TACKERS
L = CARTELS   TARCELS   (Ch only)
N = CANTERS   CARNETS   NECTARS
    RECANTS   TANRECS   (Ch only)   TRANCES
O = COATERS   COASTER
P = CARPETS
R = CARTERS   CRATERS   TRACERS
S = CASTERS
T = CATTERS   (Ch only)   SCATTER
U = CURATES   CRUSTAE   (Ch only)

41.   RESIDE

A	= DEARIES	READIES		
C	= DECRIES			
D	= DERIDES	DESIRED	RESIDED	
E	= SEEDIER			
L	= LIEDERS	(Ch only)		
D	= DENIERS		NEREIDS	
O	= OREIDES			
P	= PRESIDE	SPEIRED	(Ch only)	
R	= DESIRER	(Ch only)	RESIDER	
S	= DESIRES	RESIDES		
T	= DIETERS	(Ox only)	REISTED	(Ch only)
U	= RESIDUE	UREIDES	(Ox only)	
V	= DERIVES	REVISED		

42.   STRIDE

A	= ASTERID	(Ch only)	ASTRIDE	DISRATE
	STAIDER	STAIRED	TIRADES	
B	= BESTRID	BISTRED		
C	= CREDITS	DIRECTS		
D	= STRIDED	(Ox only)		
E	= DIETERS	(Ox only)	REISTED	(Ch only)
G	= GRISTED	(Ox only)		
H	= DITHERS	SHIRTED		
I	= DIRTIES			
K	= SKIRTED	STRIKED	(Ox only)	
N	= TINDERS			
O	= EDITORS	ROISTED	SORTIED	(Ch only)
	STEROID	(Ch only)	STORIED	TRIODES
P	= SPIRTED	STRIPED		
R	= STIRRED			
S	= STRIDES			
U	= DUSTIER	REDUITS	(Ch only)	STUDIER
V	= DIVERTS			
W	= WRISTED	(Ox only)		

43. SIGNED

A = AGNISED
E = SEEDING
I = DINGIES
L = DINGLES
N = SENDING
O = DINGOES
R = DINGERS
T = STINGED
U = SUEDING
W = SWINGED

44. STEROL

A = OESTRAL (Ch only)
B = BOLTERS LOBSTER
C = COLTERS CORSLET
D = OLDSTER STRODLE (Ch only)
F = LOFTERS
H = HOLSTER
I = LOITERS TOILERS
J = JOLTERS
L = TOLLERS
N = LENTORS
O = LOOTERS
P = PETROLS
S = STEROLS
T = SETTLOR TOLTERS (Ch only)
U = ELUTORS (Ch only) OUTLERS (Ch only)
V = REVOLTS
W = TROWELS

45.   SANDIE

69% chance using Chambers
62% chance using Oxford

A	=	NAIADES				
B	=	BANDIES				
C	=	CANDIES				
D	=	DANDIES				
A	=	ANISEED				
G	=	AGNISED	(Ch only)			
K	=	KANDIES	(Ch only)			
L	=	DENIALS	SNAILED			
M	=	DEMAINS	MEDIANS			
O	=	ADONISE	(Ch only)	ANODISE		
P	=	PANDIES	(Ch only)	SPAINED	(Ch only)	
R	=	RANDIES	(Ch only)	SANDIER	SARDINE	
T	=	DETAINS	INSTEAD	SAINTED	STAINED	
V	=	INVADES				
W	=	SWAINED	(Ox only)	DEWANIS	(Ch only)	

46.   ILLEST

69% chance using Chambers
50% chance using Oxford

A	=	TALLIES	
B	=	BILLETS	
D	=	STILLED	
E	=	TELLIES	(Ch only)
F	=	FILLETS	
G	=	GILLETS	(Ch only)
J	=	JILLETS	
I	=	ILLIEST	
K	=	SKILLET	
M	=	MILLETS	
N	=	LENTILS	
R	=	STILLER	TILLERS
S	=	LISTELS	
U	=	TUILLES	

47. CLOSER

69% chance using Chambers or Oxford

```
A  =  ESCOLAR
B  =  CORBELS
D  =  SCOLDER
E  =  CREOLES
H  =  ORCHELS    CHOLERS
I  =  RECOILS
K  =  LOCKERS
O  =  COOLERS
R  =  CLOSERS
T  =  COLTERS    CORSLET
U  =  CLOSURE    COLURES
V  =  CLOVERS
```

48. RESITE

68% chance using Chambers
73% chance using Oxford

```
A  =  AERIEST    SERIATE
B  =  REBITES
C  =  CERITES    RECITES
D  =  DIETERS    (Ox only)      REISTED    (Ch only)
E  =  EERIEST
H  =  HEISTER    (Ch only)
I  =  EIRIEST    (Ox only)
L  =  LEISTER    STERILE
M  =  METIERS    TREMISE        TRISEME
      (Ch only)  (Ch only)      (Ch only)
N  =  ENTIRES    ENTRIES        TRENISE    NERITES
                                (Ch only)
P  =  RESPITE
R  =  REITERS    RESTIER        RETIRES    RETRIES
                 (Ch only)                 (Ch only)
      TERRIES
T  =  TESTIER
U  =  SUETIER    EURITES        (Ox only)
V  =  RESTIVE    VERIEST
W  =  STEWIER
X  =  EXISTER    (Ox only)
```

49. ENTIRE

68% chance using Chambers
57% chance using Oxford

A	=	RETINAE	TRAINEE	
B	=	BENTIER		
C	=	ENTERIC	ENTICER	TERCINE	(Ox only)
E	=	TEENIER		
F	=	FEINTER		
G	=	INTEGER	TEERING	TREEING	GENTIER
H	=	ETHERIN	(Ox only)	NEITHER	THEREIN
I	=	ERINITE		
K	=	KERNITE		
N	=	INTERNE		
R	=	REINTER	RENTIER	TERRINE	
S	=	ENTIRES	ENTRIES	TRENISE	NERITES
				(Ch only)	
T	=	TENTIER	(Ch only)	
U	=	RETINUE	REUNITE	UTERINE

50. STARRED

68% chance using Chambers
65% using Oxford

C	=	REDACTS			
D	=	RADDEST	(Ch only)		
E	=	DERATES	ESTRADE	REASTED	(Ch only)
F	=	STRAFED			
H	=	DEARTHS	HARDEST	HATREDS	THREADS
		TRASHED			
I	=	ASTERID	(Ch only)	ASTRIDE	DISRATE
		STAIDER	STAIRED	TIRADES	
L	=	DARTLES			
N	=	STANDER	STERNAD	(Ox only)	
O	=	DOATERS	ROASTED		
P	=	DEPARTS			
R	=	DARTERS	STARRED		
T	=	STARTED			
W	=	STRAWED			

51.   RIVETS

67% chance using Chambers
50% chance using Oxford

A	=	TAIVERS	(Ch only)	VASTIER
D	=	DIVERTS		STRIVED	(Ch only)
E	=	RESTIVE		
G	=	GRIVETS		
H	=	THRIVES		
I	=	STIVIER	(Ch only)	
N	=	STRIVEN		
P	=	PRIVETS		
O	=	TORSIVE	(Ch only)	
S	=	STIVERS		TREVISS	(Ch only)
T	=	TRIVETS		

52.   POSTER

66% chance using chambers
64% chance using Oxford

A	=	ESPARTO		SEAPORT		
F	=	FORPETS	(Ch only)			
H	=	POTHERS		STROPHE		
I	=	PORIEST	(Ch only)	REPOSIT	RIPOSTE	
		ROPIEST				
L	=	PETROLS				
N	=	POSTERN		PRONEST		
O	=	STOOPER				
P	=	STOPPER				
R	=	PORTERS				
S	=	POSTERS				
T	=	POTTERS		SPOTTER		
U	=	POSTURE	POUTERS	SPOUTER	TROUPES	
W	=	PROWEST				
X	=	EXPORTS				

136

53. INGOTS

A = AGONIST (Ch only)
C = COSTING
D = DOTINGS
G = GESTION (Ox only)
H = HOSTING (Ox only)   TOSHING
I = TOISING (Ox only)
K = STOKING
L = LINGOTS
M = GNOMIST (Ox only)
N = STONING
O = SOOTING
P = POSTING   STOPING (Ch only)
R = STORING
S = TOSSING
T = SOTTING
U = OUSTING   OUTINGS
V = STOVING   VOTINGS
W = STOWING
Y = TOYINGS (Ch only)

A =	EASTING	EATINGS	INGESTA	SEATING
			(Ch only)	
	SIGNATE	TEASING	TSIGANE	TANGIES
			(Ch only)	(Ch only)

B =	BESTING		
D =	STINGED	NIDGETS	
H =	NIGHEST		
I =	IGNITES		
J =	JESTING		
L =	SINGLET	TINGLES	
M =	TEMSING		
N =	NESTING		
O =	GESTION	(Ox only)	
R =	RESTING	STINGER	
S =	SIGNETS		
T =	SETTING	TESTING	
U =	GUNITES	(Ch only)	
V =	VESTING		
W =	STEWING	WESTING	
Z =	ZESTING		
	(Ox only)		

55. SAINER

66% chance using Chambers
59% chance using Oxford

C	= ARSENIC	CARNIES	CERASIN	
D	= RANDIES	(Ch only)	SANDIER	SARDINE
F	= INFARES			
G	= ERASING	GAINERS	REGAINS	SEARING
	SERINGA	(Ch only)		
H	= ARSHINE	(Ch only)	HERNIAS	
I	= SENARII	(Ch only)		
K	= SNAKIER			
L	= ALINERS	LAINERS	NAILERS	
	(Ox only)	(Ox only)		
M	= MARINES	REMAINS	SEMINAR	
N	= INSNARE	(Ch only)		
O	= ERASION			
P	= PANSIER	(Ch only)	RAPINES	
R	= SIERRAN	SNARIER		
S	= ARSINES			
T	= NASTIER	RATINES	RESIANT	RESTAIN
	RETINAS	RETSINA	STAINER	RETAINS
	STARNIE	(Ch only)	(see STERN)	STEARIN
U	= ANURIES	(Ox only)		
V	= RAVINES			
W	= WAINERS	(Ox only)		
Z	= REZINAS	(Ox only)		

56.   INSTEP

A = PANTIES   SAPIENT   SPINATE   (Ch only)
C = INSPECT   PECTINES
D = STIPEND
I = PINIEST
K = PINKEST
L = PINTLES
N = PINNETS   (Ch only)   TENPINS   (Ch only)
O = PONTIES   (see PUNTY)
P = SNIPPET
R = NIPTERS   PTERINS   TERPINS
    (Ch only)   (Ch only)   (Ox only)
S = INSTEPS   SPINETS
T = SPINNET
U = PUNIEST   PUNTIES

57.   CANTER

A = CATERAN
D = CANTRED   TRANCED
E = CRENATE
F = CANTREF
H = CHANTER   TRANCHE   (Ch only)
I = CERTAIN   CITREAN   CRINATE
    NACRITE   (Ch only)   CANTIER   (Ch only)
L = CENTRAL
O = ENACTOR   ORCANET   (Ox only)
P = CARPENT   (Ox only)
S = CANTERS   CARNETS   NECTARS   TRANCES
    RECANTS
U = CAUNTER   CENTAUR   UNCRATE
Y = ENCRATY   (Ch only)   NECTARY

58. LESTER

```
A  =  ELATERS    REALEST    RELATES    STEALER
B  =  BELTERS    TREBLES
C  =  TERCELS
F  =  FELTERS
G  =  REGLETS    (Ch only)
H  =  SHELTER
I  =  LEISTER    STERILE
K  =  KELTERS    KESTREL
L  =  TELLERS
M  =  MELTERS    SMELTER
N  =  RELENTS
P  =  PETRELS    SPELTER
S  =  STREELS
T  =  LETTERS    STERLET
V  =  SVELTER
S  =  SWELTER    WELTERS
Y  =  TERSELY
Z  =  SELTZER
```

59. TINGER

```
A  =  GRANITE    INGRATE    TEARING
E  =  GENTIER    INTEGER    TEERING    TREEING
I  =  IGNITER    TIERING
J  =  JERTING    (Ox only)
L  =  RINGLET    TINGLER    TRINGLE
M  =  METRING
N  =  RENTING    RINGENT
O  =  GENITOR    TRIGONE
S  =  RESTING    STINGER
T  =  GITTERN    RETTING
V  =  VERTING
```

60. RAINED

65% chance using Chambers
41% chance using Oxford

A = ARANEID (Ch only)
B = BRAINED
D = DANDIER DRAINED
G = AREDING EARDING (Ch only) GRADINE
    GRAINED READING
H = HANDIER
I = DENARII
M = DIMERAN MARINED INARMED ADERMIN
    (Ox only) (Ox only) (Ch only) (Ch only)
O = ANEROID
P = PARDINE (Ch only)
R = RANDIER (Ch only)
S = RANDIES (Ch only) SANDIER SARDINE
T = DETRAIN TRAINED
U = UNAIRED
V = RAVINED

61. SINLED

64% chance using Chambers
50% chance using Oxford

A = DENIALS
D = DINDLES
E = ENISLED LINSEED
I = INISLED
K = KINDLES
M = MILDENS
N = DINNLES (Ch only)
O = SONDELI (Ch only)
P = SPINDLE
T = DENTILS
W = SWINDLE WINDLES

62. BATING

A = ABATING
B = TABBING
E = BEATING
H = BATHING
I = BAITING
L = TABLING
N = BANTING
O = BOATING
S = BASTING
T = BATTING

63. LOPERS

A = PAROLES
D = POLDERS
E = LEPROSE
G = PROLEGS   (Ch only)
I = SLOPIER   SPOILER   (Ch only)
L = POLLERS
O = LOOPERS   SPOOLER
P = LOPPERS
T = PETROLS
U = LEPROUS   PELORUS   (Ch only)

64. PASTER

A =	PETARAS	(Ch only)		
C =	CARPETS	SPECTRA		
D =	DEPARTS			
H =	TERAPHS	(Ox only)	THREAPS	SPARTHE
I =	PARTIES	PASTIER	PIASTRE	PIASTER
	PIRATES	TRAIPSE		
L =	PALTERS	PLASTER	PLATERS	STAPLER
M =	TAMPERS	STAMPER		
N =	ARPENTS	ENTRAPS	PANTERS	PARENTS
	(Ch only)	PASTERN		
O =	ESPARTO	SEAPORT		
P =	TAPPERS			
P =	PASTERS	REPASTS		
T =	PATTERS	SPATTER		
U =	PASTURE			

65.   ASCENT

63% chance using Chambers
54% chance using Oxford

```
A = CATENAS   (Ch only)
H = NATCHES   CHASTEN
I = CANIEST   CINEAST   (Ch only)
K = NACKETS   (Ch only)
L = CANTLES
N = NASCENT
O = COSTEAN
R = CANTERS   NECTARS   RECANTS   SCANTER
S = ASCENTS   STANCES
```

66.   STABLE

63% chance using Chambers
55% chance using Oxford

```
A = ASTABLE   (Ch only)
D = BLASTED   STABLED
E = BELATES
I = STABILE
L = BALLETS
O = OBLATES
R = BLASTER   STABLER
S = STABLES
T = BATTELS   BATTLES   TABLETS
```

67. THEIRS

A = HASTIER   SHERIAT   (Ch only)
B = HERBIST   (Ch only)
C = CITHERS   RICHEST
D = DITHERS
E = HEISTER   (Ch only)
F = SHIFTER
G = SIGHTER
H = HITHERS   (Ch only)
L = SLITHER
M = HERMITS
N = HINTERS   (Ox only)
O = HORIEST
P = HIPSTER
T = HITTERS
U = HIRSUTE
V = THRIVES
W = WITHERS   WRITHES
Z = ZITHERS

68. SINGLE

A = LEASING   SEALING
D = DINGLES   SINGLED
F = SELFING   (Ch only)
G = GINGLES   SNIGGLE
H = SHINGLE
I = SEILING   (Ch only)
J = JINGLES
L = LINGELS   LINGLES   SELLING
M = MINGLES
P = PINGLES   (Ch only)   SPIGNEL
R = SINGLER   SLINGER
S = SINGLES
T = SINGLET   TINGLES
U = LUNGIES   (Ch only)   SLUEING
W = SLEWING

69. ANGLER

61% chance using Chambers
58% chance using Oxford

A = ALNAGER
B = BRANGLE
C = CLANGER
D = DANGLER GNARLED
E = ENLARGE GENERAL GLEANER
I = ENGRAIL LEARING REGINAL REALIGN
      NARGILE (Ch only) (Ch only)
M = MANGLER (Ch only)
S = ANGLERS LARGENS
T = TANGLER TRANGLE (Ch only)
U = UNREGAL ULNAGER
W = WRANGLE (Ch only)

70. RESTED

61% chance using Chambers
59% chance using Oxford

A = DEAREST DERATES ESTRADE REASTED
                                    (Ch only)
C = CRESTED
D = REDDEST TEDDERS
E = REESTED (Ch only) STEERED
I = DIETERS (Ch only) REISTED (Ch only)
N = TENDERS STERNED
O = OERSTED ROSETED TEREDOS
                (Ch only) (Ox only)
S = DESERTS TRESSED
V = VERDETS (Ch only)
W = STREWED
X = DEXTERS

71. CHEATS

B	=	BATCHES		
C	=	CACHETS	CATCHES	
D	=	SCATHED		
E	=	ESCHEAT	TEACHES	
H	=	HATCHES		
I	=	AITCHES		
H	=	HACKEST		
L	=	LATCHES	SATCHEL	
M	=	MATCHES		
N	=	CHASTEN	NATCHES	
P	=	PATCHES		
R	=	CHASTER	RATCHES	ARCHEST
S	=	SACHETS	SCATHES	
W	=	WATCHES		

72. MANGES

A	=	MANAGES		
E	=	MANEGES	(Ch only)	MENAGES
I	=	GAMINES	MEASING	SEAMING
		(Ch only)	(Ch only)	
L	=	MANGLES		
O	=	MANGOES		
R	=	ENGRAMS	GERMANS	MANGERS
T	=	MAGNETS		
W	=	SWAGMEN	(Ch only)	

73. TOILES

A = ISOLATE
C = CITOLES
H = HOLIEST
I = OILIEST
N = ENTOILS
O = OOLITES   OSTIOLE
P = PISTOLE
T = TOILERS   LOITERS
T = LITOTES   TOILETS
U = OUTLIES
V = OLIVETS   VIOLETS

74. RATONS

A = TORANAS   (Ch only)
C = CARTONS
E = ATONERS   SENATOR   TREASON
I = AROINTS   RATIONS
M = MATRONS
O = RATOONS
P = TARPONS
T = RATTONS
U = SANTOUR   (Ch only)
Y = AROYNTS   (see AROINT)

75. BRIDES

A = BRAISED
C = SCRIBED
D = BIDDERS
G = BRIDGES
I = BIRDIES
L = BRIDLES
N = BINDERS   REBINDS
O = DISROBE
T = BESTRID   BISTRED
U = BRUISED

76. THRACE

```
A = TRACHEA   (Ch only)
C = CATCHER
D = CHARTED
H = HATCHER
I = THERIAC   (Ch only)
L = ARCHLET
M = MATCHER
N = CHANTER
P = CHAPTER   PATCHER
R = CHARTER
S = CHASTER   RATCHES   ARCHEST
T = CHATTER   RATCHET
W = WATCHER
```

77. PINGLE

```
A = LEAPING   PEALING
D = PINGLED   (Ch only)
E = PEELING
H = HELPING
O = ELOPING
P = LEPPING
R = PINGLER   (Ch only)
S = PINGLES   (Ch only)   SPIGNEL
T = PELTING
Y = YELPING
```

78. CANERS

```
C = CANCERS
D = DANCERS
E = CAREENS
H = ENARCHS   (Ch only)
I = ARSENIC   CARNIES   CERASIN
L = LANCERS
N = CANNERS   SCANNER
O = CARNOSE
P = PRANCES
T = CANTERS   CARNETS   NECTARS   RECANTS
    TRANCES
```

79.　REGAIN

58% chance using Chambers
49% using Oxford

B	= BEARING			
D	= AREDING	EARDING	GRAINED	READING
		(Ch only)		GRADINE
F	= FEARING			
G	= GEARING			
H	= HEARING			
L	= ENGRAIL	LEARING	NARGILE	REALIGN
		(Ch only)	(Ch only)	(Ch only)
	REGINAL			
M	= MANGIER	REAMING		
N	= GERANIN	(Ch only)	GRANNIE	NEARING
O	= ORIGANE	(Ch only)		
P	= REAPING			
R	= EARRING	GRAINER	RANGIER	REARING
S	= EARINGS	ERASING	GAINERS	REGAINS
	SEARING	SERINGA	(Ch only)	
T	= GRANITE	INGRATE	TEARING	
V	= REAVING	VINEGAR		
W	= WEARING			

80.　STRAIN

57% chance using Chambers
51% chance using Oxford

A	= ANTIARS	ARTISAN	TSARINA	
	(Ch only)		(Ox only)	
E	= NASTIER	RATINES	RESIANT	RESTAIN
	RETAINS	RETINAS	RETSINA	STAINER
	STARNIE	(Ch only:	see STERN)	STEARIN
G	= RATINGS	STARING		
H	= TARNISH			
L	= RATLINS			
M	= MARTINS			
O	= AROINTS	RATIONS		
P	= SPRAINT	(Ch only)		
S	= INSTARS	SANTIRS	(Ch only)	STRAINS
T	= STRAINT	(Ox only)	TRANSIT	
U	= NUTRIAS	(Ch only)		

81. RUSTLE

```
A = SALUTER
B = BLUSTER
C = CLUSTER
D = LUSTRED     RUSTLED
F = FLUSTER
H = HURTLES     HUSTLER
I = LUSTIER     RULIEST
N = RUNLETS
R = RUSTLER
S = LUSTRES     RESULTS     RUSTLES     SUTLERS
T = TURTLES
Y = SUTLERY
```

82. GARNET

```
A = TANAGER     (Ch only)
D = GRANTED
E = GRANTEE     GREATEN     REAGENT
I = GRANITE     INGRATE     TEARING
L = TANGLER     TRANGLE     (Ch only)
M = GARMENT     MARGENT
O = TRONAGE     (Ox only)
R = GRANTER     REGRANT
S = ARGENTS     GARNETS     STRANGE
U = GAUNTER
```

                N.B. This one takes all the vowels

83.   SCRINE

A = ARSENIC   CARNIES   CERASIN
D = CINDERS   DISCERN
E = SINCERE
G = CRINGES   SCRINGE
H = RICHENS
K = NICKERS   SNICKER
M = MINCERS
O = COINERS   CRINOSE   (Ch only)   CRONIES
    ORCEINS   ORCINES   SERICON   (Ch only)
P = PINCERS   PRINCES
S = RINCES   (Ox only)
T = CISTERN   CRETINS
W = WINCERS

84.   PESTER

A = REPEATS   SPERATE   (Ox only)
C = RECEPTS   RESPECT   SCEPTRE   SPECTRE
    (Ch only)
E = ESTREPE   STEEPER
H = THREEPS   (Ch only)
I = RESPITE
L = PELTERS
N = PRESENT   REPENTS   SERPENT
S = PESTERS
T = PETTERS   (Ch only)
X = EXPERTS

85. EALING

B	=	BLEAING	(Ox only)	
C	=	ANGELIC		
D	=	ALIGNED	DEALING	LEADING
E	=	LINEAGE		
F	=	FEALING	(Ch only)	FINAGLE	LEAFING
G	=	LIGNAGE	(Ch only)	
H	=	HEALING		
K	=	LEAKING		
L	=	GALLEIN	(Ox only)	
M	=	LEAMING	(Ch only)	MEALING
N	=	LEANING	NEALING	ANELING
P	=	LEAPING	PEALING	
R	=	ENGRAIL	LEARING	NARGILE	REALIGN
			(Ch only)	(Ch only)	(Ch only)
		REGINAL		
S	=	LEASING	SEALING	
T	=	ELATING	GELATIN	GENITAL
V	=	LEAVING		

86. RINGED

A	=	AREDING	EARDING	(Ch only)	GRADINE
		GRAINED	READING	
B	=	BREDING		
C	=	CRINGED		
E	=	REEDING	REIGNED	
F	=	FRINGED		
I	=	DINGIER		
L	=	GRINDLE	(Ox only)	
N	=	RENDING		
O	=	GROINED	NEGROID	
S	=	DINGERS	(Ch only)	

87.   MARINE

A	=	AMARINE	(Ox only)	
C	=	CARMINE		
D	=	DIMERAN	MARINED	INARMED	ADERMIN
		(Ox only)	(Ox only)	(Ch only)	(Ch only)
E	=	REMANIE	(Ch only)	
G	=	MANGIER	REAMING	MEARING	(Ox only)
H	=	HARMINE		
K	=	RAMEKIN		
L	=	MANLIER	MARLINE	RAILMEN	(Ch only)
O	=	MORAINE		
R	=	MARINER		
S	=	MARINES	REMAINS	SEMINAR
T	=	MINARET	RAIMENT	

88.   LACING

E	=	ANGELIC
K	=	LACKING
L	=	CALLING
M	=	CALMING
N	=	LANCING
O	=	COALING
P	=	PLACING
S	=	LACINGS
T	=	CATLING
U	=	GLUCINA
W	=	CLAWING
Y	=	CLAYING

89.   ALBERT

A	=	RATABLE	
E	=	RETABLE	
H	=	BLATHER	HALBERT
I	=	LIBRATE	TRIABLE
O	=	BLOATER	
S	=	BLASTER	STABLER
T	=	BATTLER	
W	=	BLEWART	(Ch only)

90. INVEST

55% chance using chambers
43% chance using Oxford

```
A = NAIVEST    NATIVES    VAINEST
E = VENITES    (Ch only)
G = VESTING
I = VINIEST
L = VENTILS
N = INVENTS
R = INVERTS    STRIVEN
S = INVESTS
```

91. UNITER

55% chance using Chambers or Oxford

```
A = RUINATE    TAURINE    URANITE    URINATE
B = TRIBUNE    TURBINE
D = INTRUDE    TURDINE    (Ch only)    UNTRIED
E = RETINUE    REUNITE    UTERINE
G = TRUEING
R = RUNTIER
S = TRIUNES    UNITERS
T = NUTTIER
V = VENTURI    (Ch only)    UNRIVET
W = UNWRITE
```

92. SECRET

55% chance using Chambers or Oxford

```
A = CREATES    SECRETA    (Ch only)
D = CRESTED
E = SECRETE
H = RETCHES
I = CERITES    RECITES
L = TERCELS
N = CENTRES
P = RECEPTS    RESPECT    SCEPTRE    SPECTRE
    (Ch only)
S = CRESSET    SECRETS
```

93. NOSIER

A	=	ERASION		
C	=	COINERS	CRINOSE (Ch only)	CRONIES
		ORCEINS	ORCINES	SERICON (Ch only)
D	=	INDORSE	ROSINED	SORDINE
F	=	FERISON (Ox only)		
G	=	ERINGOS	REGIONS	
H	=	INSHORE		
I	=	IRONIES	NOISIER	
L	=	LIENORS	NEROLIS	RESINOL	SEROLIN
		(Ox only)		(Ox only)	(Ox only)
P	=	ORPINES	PIONERS	
R	=	IRONERS		
S	=	SONERIS (Ch only)	SONSIER	
T	=	ORIENTS	STONIER	TERSION (Ch only)	TRIONES (Ch only)
X	=	OREXINS (Ox only)		

94. UTTERS

A	=	AUSTERE	
B	=	BUTTERS	
C	=	CUTTERS	
D	=	TRUSTED	
G	=	GUTTERS	
H	=	SHUTTER	
M	=	MUTTERS	
N	=	ENTRUST	NUTTERS
O	=	STOUTER	TOUTERS
P	=	PUTTERS	SPUTTER
R	=	RUTTERS	TRUSTER
T	=	STUTTER	

95. RAGING

B = BARGING
C = GRACING
D = GRADING NIGGARD
E = GEARING
L = GLARING
N = RANGING
S = RAGINGS
T = GRATING
V = GRAVING
Y = GRAYING
Z = GRAZING

96. PARSON

D = PARDONS
E = PERSONA (Ch only)
I = SOPRANI
O = SOPRANO PRONAOS (Ch only)
R = SPORRAN
S = PARSONS SPORANS (Ox only)
T = PATRONS TARPONS

97. TANGLE

B = BANGLET
D = TANGLED
E = ANGELET (Ox only)   ELEGANT
I = ELATING GELATIN GENITAL
O = ANGELOT (Ox only)   TANGELO (Ch only)
R = TANGLER TRANGLE (Ch only)
S = TANGLES
U = GLUTEAN LANGUET

157

98.   CANDLE

A = CANDELA   (Ch only)
D = CANDLED
E = CLEANED   ELANCED   ENLACED
G = GLANCED   CLANGED
I = INLACED
S = CANDLES
T = CANTLED
U = UNLACED

N.B. The usable letters make GAUDEST so make a mental image of the GAUDIEST CANDLE you can imagine.

99.   ARMING

B = BARMING
E = MANGIER   REAMING
F = FARMING
H = HARMING
K = MARKING
L = MARLING
M = RAMMING
N = RINGMAN   (Ch only)
P = RAMPING
R = MARRING
S = MARGINS
T = MIGRANT
W = WARMING

100.   IDATES

E = IDEATES
L = DETAILS   DILATES
M = MISDATE
N = DETAINS   INSTEAD   SATINED   STAINED
O = IODATES
R = STAIDER   STAIRED   ASTRIDE   DISRATE
S = DISSEAT
U = DAUTIES   (Ch only)
V = DATIVES
W = DAWTIES   (Ch only)   WAISTED

101. RATTEN

54% chance using
Chambers or Oxford

A	= TARTANE			
E	= ENTREAT	RATTEEN	TERNATE	
I	= ITERANT	(Ch only)	NATTIER	NITRATE
	TERTIAN	TARTINE		
N	= ENTRANT			
P	= PATTERN			
R	= TRANTER			
S	= RATTENS			
U	= TAUNTER			

102. GRATES

53% chance using Chambers
41% chance using Oxford

E	= ERGATES	(Ch only)		
G	= STAGGER			
H	= GATHERS			
I	= AGISTER	GAITERS	STAGIER	STRIGAE
	TRIAGES		(Ch only)	
N	= ARGENTS	GARNETS	STRANGE	
O	= STORAGE	ORGEATS		
P	= PARGETS			
R	= GARRETS			
Y	= GRAYEST	GYRATES	STAGERY	

103. LEARNS

53% chance using Chambers
50% chance using Oxford

A	= ARSENAL			
B	= BRANSLE	(Ch only)		
C	= LANCERS	RANCELS	(Ch only)	
D	= LANDERS	SLANDER	DARNELS	
F	= SALFERN	(Ch only)		
G	= ANGLERS			
I	= ALINERS	LAINERS	NAILERS	
	(Ox only)	(Ox only)		
K	= RANKLES			
N	= LANNERS			
P	= PLANNERS			
S	= RANSELS	(Ch only)		
T	= ALTERNS	ANTLERS	RENTALS	STERNAL
U	= AULNERS	(Ox only: see ALNAGER)		

104. SPANED

53% chance using Chambers
33% chance using Oxford

```
E  =  SPEANED     (Ch only)
G  =  SPANGED
I  =  PANDIES     PANSIED       SPAINED
      (Ch only)                 (Ch only)
K  =  SPANKED
M  =  DAMPENS
N  =  SPANNED
O  =  DAPSONE     (Ch only)
P  =  SNAPPED
R  =  PANDERS
W  =  SPAWNED
X  =  EXPANDS
```

105. ANGLES

53% chance using Chambers
55% chance using Oxford

```
A  =  ALNAGES
B  =  BANGLES
C  =  GLANCES
D  =  DANGLES     SLANGED
F  =  FLANGES
I  =  LEASING     SEALING
J  =  JANGLES
M  =  MANGLES
P  =  SPANGLE
R  =  ANGLERS
S  =  GLASSEN
T  =  TANGLES
U  =  ULNAGES     (Ox only)
W  =  WANGLES
```

106. METIER

A = EMIRATE   MEATIER
D = DEMERIT   MERITED
E = EREMITE
I = EMERITI   (Ch only)
P = EMPTIER   (N.B. This is a noun)
R = TRIREME
S = METIERS   TREMIES   TRISEME
       (Ch only)   (Ch only)   (Ch only)
T = TERMITE

107. NAMERS

E = RENAMES
G = ENGRAMS   GERMANS   MANGERS
I = MARINES   REMAINS   SEMINAR
N = MANNERS
O = OARSMEN
T = MARTENS   SARMENT   SMARTEN
U = MANURES   MURENAS   SURNAME

108. REVISE

C = SERVICE
D = REVISED
E = VEERIES
G = GRIEVES
L = REVILES   SERVILE
N = INVERSE   VERSINE   (Ch only)
P = PREVISE
R = REIVERS   REVISER
S = REVISES
T = STIEVER   (Ch only)   VERIEST

161

109. ROISED

52% chance using Chambers or Oxford

A	=	SOREDIA		
B	=	DISROBE		
D	=	SODDIER		
I	=	OSIERED		
L	=	SOLDIER	SOLIDER	
M	=	MISDOER	MOIDERS	
N	=	INDORSE	ROSINED	SORDINE
S	=	DOSSIER		
T	=	EDITORS	ROISTED	ROSITED	SORTIED
			(Ch only)	(Ch only)	
		STEROID	(Ch only)	STORIED	TRIODES
V	=	DEVISOR	DEVOIRS	VISORED
W	=	DOWRIES	ROWDIES	

110. PRISER

52% chance using Chambers or Oxford

A	=	PARRIES	PRAISER	REPAIRS
C	=	CRISPER		
E	=	PERRIES	REPRISE	RESPIRE
G	=	GRIPERS		
I	=	SPIRIER		
P	=	RIPPERS		
O	=	PROSIER		
U	=	PURSIER		
Z	=	PRIZERS		

111. ARMIES

52% chance using Chambers
50% chance using Oxford

B	=	AMBRIES		
D	=	MARDIES (Ch only: see MAR)	MISREAD	
E	=	SEAMIER		
H	=	MISHEAR		
L	=	MAILERS	(Ch only)	REALISM
P	=	SAMPIRE	(Ch only)	
N	=	MARINES	SEMINAR	REMAINS
R	=	MARRIES		
S	=	MASSIER		
T	=	MAISTER	MASTIER	(Ch only)	MISRATE
W	=	AWMRIES	(Ch only)	

112.   ENTAIL

51% chance using Chambers
54% chance using Oxford

A	=	ANTLIAE	(Ch only)	LANIATE	(Ox only)
E	=	ELATINE	(Ox only)	LINEATE	
F	=	INFLATE			
G	=	ELATING	GELATIN	GENITAL	
M	=	AILMENT	ALIMENT		
O	=	ELATION			
P	=	PANTILE			
R	=	ENTRAIL	LATRINE	RATLINE	RELIANT
		RETINAL	TRENAIL		
S	=	ELASTIN	ENTAILS	SALIENT	
		STANIEL	(Ch only)	TENAILS	(Ch only)
V	=	VENTAIL	(Ox only)		

113.   MARION

51% chance using Chambers
20% chance using Oxford

E	=	MORAINE	
C	=	MARCONI	
G	=	ROAMING	
I	=	AMORINI	(Ch only)
O	=	AMORINO	(Ch only)
S	=	MAINORS	(Ch only)
T	=	TORMINA	(Ch only)
U	=	MAINOUR	(Ch only)

114.   SIMPER

50% chance using Chambers
30% chance using Oxford

A	=	SAMPIRE	(Ch only)	
E	=	EMPIRES	EMPRISE	PREMISE
I	=	PRIMSIE	(Ch only)	
L	=	PRELIMS	(Ch only)	
S	=	IMPRESS	SIMPERS	
T	=	IMPREST	PERMITS	PRIMEST
U	=	UMPIRES		

115. RUDIES

50% chance using Chambers
48% chance using Oxford

A = RESIDUA
C = DISCURE   (Ch only)
D = RUDDIES
E = RESIDUE
H = HURDIES
N = INSURED
Q = SQUIRED
T = DUSTIER   REDUITS   (Ch only)   STUDIER
R = DRUSIER

116. SORDIN

50% chance using Chambers
34% chance using Oxford

A = INROADS   ORDAINS
E = INDORSE   ROSINED   SORDINE
G = RODINGS   (Ch only)
H = SORDINI   (Ch only)
O = INDOORS   SORDINO   (Ch only)
U = DURIONS   (Ch only)

117. BONDER

50% chance using
Chambers or Oxford

A = BANDORE
E = ENROBED
I = INORBED
L = BLONDER
S = BONDERS
U = BOUNDER   REBOUND   UNROBED
W = BROWNED
Z = BRONZED

118. RELATE

50% chance using Chambers
27% chance using Oxford

```
A  =  LAETARE    (Ch only)
B  =  RETABLE
D  =  RELATED
F  =  REFLATE    (Ch only)
I  =  ATELIER    (Ch only)
N  =  ALTERNE    ENTERAL    ETERNAL    TENERAL
      (Ch only)
P  =  PRELATE
R  =  RELATER
S  =  ELATERS    REALEST    RELATES    STEALER
X  =  EXALTER
```

119. STRERT

50% chance using Chambers
40% chance using Oxford

```
A  =  STARTER
E  =  TERRETS
I  =  TERRITS
O  =  TORRETS    (Ch only)
U  =  TURRETS
Y  =  TRYSTER
```

120. ANGERS

49% chance using
Chambers or Oxford

```
B  =  BANGERS
D  =  DANGERS
G  =  GANGERS
H  =  HANGERS
I  =  ERASING    GAINERS    REGAINS    SEARING
      SERINGA    (Ch only)
L  =  ANGLERS    LARGENS
M  =  MANGERS
O  =  ONAGERS    ORANGES
R  =  RANGERS
T  =  ARGENTS    GARNETS    STRANGE
```

121. SOUTER

```
C = SCOUTER
D = DETOURS    DOUTERS    OUTREDS    (Ch only)
    ROUSTED
H = SHOUTER    SOUTHER
I = TOUSIER
L = ELUTORS    (Ch only)              OUTLERS    (Ch only)
M = MOUTERS    (Ch only)
N = TONSURE
P = PETROUS    POSTURE    POUTERS    SPOUTER
    TROUPES    SEPTUOR
R = RETOURS    ROUSTER    ROUTERS    TOURERS
    (Ch only)  (Ch only)
S = OESTRUS    (Ch only)  OUSTERS    SOUREST
    SOUTERS    TOUSERS    TROUSES    TUSSORE
T = STOUTER    TOUTERS
```

122. CARIES

```
B = ASCRIBE    CARIBES
D = RADICES    SIDECAR    (Ch only)
H = CASHIER
L = CLARIES    SCALIER
N = ARSENIC    CARNIES    SERACIN
O = ORACIES
E = CARRIES    SCARIER
T = RACIEST
U = URICASE    (Ch only)
V = CARVIES    VISCERA    (Ch only)    VARICES
```

123.   METALS

47% chance using Chambers
39% chance using Oxford

A = MALATES   MALTASE   (Ch only)
C = CALMEST
L = MALLETS
N = LAMENTS   MANTELS   MANTLES
O = MALTOSE
P = AMPLEST
R = ARMLETS   MARLEST   MARTELS
S = SAMLETS
U = AMULETS

124.   MANGLE

47% chance using Chambers
32% chance using Oxford

A = GAMELAN   (Ch only)
D = MANGLED
E = GLEEMAN   MELANGE
I = MEALING   LEAMING
R = MANGLER   (Ch only)
S = MANGLES

125.   CILATE

46% chance using Chambers
54% chance using Oxford

B = CITABLE
D = CITADEL   DELTAIC   EDICTAL
G = ALGETIC   (Ox only)
I = CILIATE
M = CLIMATE
O = ALOETIC   COALITE   (Ch only)
P = PLICATE
R = ARTICLE   RECITAL
S = ELASTIC   LACIEST
T = TACTILE
U = AULETIC   (Ox only)

126.　　LIMENS

A	=	ISLEMAN	MENIALS
D	=	MILDENS	
E	=	ISLEMEN	
G	=	MINGLES	
O	=	MOLINES	
R	=	MERLINS	LIMNERS
U	=	LUMINES	

127.　　SILVER

A	=	REVISAL	
C	=	CLIVERS	
E	=	REVILES	SERVILE
M	=	VERMILS	
N	=	SILVERN	
O	=	OLIVERS	VIOLERS
S	=	SILVERS	SLIVERS
Y	=	SILVERY	

128.　　SUITER

B	=	BUSTIER		
C	=	CUITERS	(Ch only)	
D	=	DUSTIER	REDUITS	STUDIER
F	=	FUSTIER		
G	=	GUSTIER		
H	=	HIRSUTE		
L	=	LUSTIER	RULIEST	
M	=	MUSTIER		
N	=	TRIUNES	UNITERS	
O	=	OURIEST	(Ch only)	
Q	=	REQUITS	(Ch only)	QUERIST
R	=	RUSTIER		

129. SEARED

G = GREASED
H = SHEARED
I = DEARIES   READINGS
L = DEALERS   LEADERS
M = SMEARED   REMADES   (Ch only)
O = OREADES   (Ch only)
P = SPEARED
R = READERS
T = DEAREST   DERATES   REASTED   (Ch only)

130. STREET

A = ESTREAT   RESTATE
B = BETTERS
E = TEETERS
F = FETTERS
L = LETTERS   STERLET
N = TENTERS
R = TERRETS
S = SETTERS   STREETS
W = WETTERS   (Ox only)

131. TAILER

B = LIBRATE   TRIABLE
C = ARTICLE   RECITAL
D = DILATER   TRAILED
L = LITERAL
M = LAMITER   MALTIER   MARLITE
N = ENTRAIL   LATRINE   RATLINE   RELIANT
    RETINAL   TRENAIL
P = PLAITER   PARTILE   (Ox only)
R = TRAILER
S = REALIST   RETAILS   SALTIER   SALTIRE
    SLATIER
T = TERTIAL
U = LAURITE   (Ox only)
W = WALTIER
Y = IRATELY   REALITY

132.   NOTICE

A	=	ACONITE	ANOETIC
L	=	LECTION	
M	=	ENTOMIC	
N	=	ENTONIC	(Ox only)
O	=	COONTIE	
P	=	ENTOPIC	NEPOTIC
R	=	CRETION	RECTION
S	=	NOTICES	SECTION
T	=	ENTOTIC	
X	=	EXCITON	(Ch only)

133.   QUEEST

A	=	EQUATES	
B	=	BEQUEST	
D	=	QUESTED	
E	=	SQUETEE	
N	=	SEQUENT	
R	=	REQUEST	QUESTER
S	=	QUEESTS	

134.   TRIPED

A	=	PIRATED			
I	=	RIPTIDE	(Ch only)		
L	=	TRIPLED			
N	=	PRINTED			
O	=	DIOPTER	DIOPTRE	PERIDOT	PROTEID
S	=	SPIRTED	STRIPED		

135.   MAGNET

A	=	MAGENTA	MAGNATE
I	=	TEAMING	MINTAGE
O	=	MAGNETO	MEGATON
R	=	GARMENT	MARGENT
S	=	MAGNETS	
U	=	MUTAGEN	(Ch only)

136. STRIFE

42% chance using Chambers or Oxford

```
A  =  FAIREST
I  =  FISTIER      (Ch only)
L  =  FILTERS      LIFTERS      TRIFLES
N  =  SNIFTER
S  =  STRIFES
T  =  FITTERS      TITFERS      (Ch only)
U  =  FUSTIER
```

137. SPIDER

42% chance using Chambers or Oxford

```
A  =  ASPIRED      DIAPERS      PRAISED      DESPAIR
C  =  DISCERP
E  =  PRESIDE      SPEIRED      (Ch only)
N  =  PINDERS
P  =  DIPPERS
S  =  SPIDERS
T  =  SPIRTED      STRIPED
```

138. NATURE

42% chance using Chambers
40% chance using Oxford

```
C  =  CAUNTER      CENTAUR      UNCRATE
D  =  NATURED      UNRATED
G  =  GAUNTER
H  =  HAUNTER
I  =  RUINATE      TAURINE      URANITE      URINATE
L  =  NEUTRAL
M  =  TRUEMAN      (Ch only)
S  =  AUNTERS      (Ch only)      NATURES      SAUNTER
T  =  TAUNTER
W  =  UNWATER
```

139. TONIES

A = ATONIES
C = NOTICES   SECTION
D = DITONES
I = INOSITE   (Ox only)
L = ENTOILS
N = INTONES
R = ORIENTS   STONIER   TERSION   (Ch only)
    TRIONES
T = TONITES
W = TOWNIES   (Ch only)

140. GIRDLE

A = GLADIER   GRAILED   (see GRAVEL)
D = GRIDDLE
L = GRILLED
N = GRINDLE   (Ox only)
O = GOLDIER
R = GIRDLER
S = GILDERS   GIRDLES   GLIDERS   GRISLED
    LIDGERS
U = GUILDER

You will observe that with the last word, GIRDLE, the odds of obtaining a seventh letter to constitute a seven-letter word dropped to about a six to four chance against you. Below this point you must consider seriously whether the risk you are taking by holding out for a fitting seventh letter to make a seven-letter word is worth it, depending on the state of the board and possibilities available of using the letters you have in smaller combinations. It is always worthwhile knowing even the least hopeful of the possibilities for seven-letter words, however, because if your use of smaller combinations of the letters you have is unduly restricted, it may well be worth taking the two to one or greater odds against you in order to try for a seven-letter word as a distinct bonus chance when there is little scoring alternative.

You now know all I can tell you about how to play better Scrabble; the rest is up to you. Not everyone can become a champion, or even wants to – but if you follow the hints I have given and always try to play openly and constructively, you will find yourself playing happier and more skilful games.

Seven-letter words becoming eight-letter words

F,ADDLING	H,ALTERED	A,WAITING	B,LIGHTED
P,ADDLING	P,ALTERED	A,WANTING	F,LIGHTED
R,ADDLING	A,BETTING	AXILLAR,Y	S,LIGHTED
S,ADDLING	A,BATABLE	A,ZYMITES	B,LIGHTER
W,ADDLING	A,BUTMENT	B,AILMENT	S,LIGHTER
M,AIDLESS	A,BUTTING	B,ANTINGS	B,LIMBING
F,AIRIEST	A,BEARING	P,ANTINGS	C,LIMBING
H,AIRIEST	A,BOUNDED	W,ANTINGS	B,LINKING
L,AIRIEST	A,BRAIDED	B,ARTISAN	C,LINKING
H,AIRLESS	A,DEEMING	B,ATONING	S,LINKING
F,AIRINGS	A,DYNAMIC	B,EARINGS	B,LITHELY
L,AIRINGS	A,GLITTER	G,EARINGS	B,LOOMING
P,AIRINGS	A,GRAPHIC	H,EARINGS	G,LOOMING
F,ALLOWED	A,GREEING,	S,EARINGS	B,LUFFING
H,ALLOWED	A,GUISING,	T,EARINGS	B,LUNTING
T,ALLOWED	A,LIGHTED	B,EARDING	B,LUSHERS
W,ALLOWED	A,LOGICAL	Y,EARDING	B,LUSHING
D,ALLYING	A,MENDING	B,EERIEST	B,LUSTERS
R,ALLYING	A,MASSING	L,EERIEST	C,LUSTERS
G,AMBLING	A,MISSING	P,EERIEST	F,LUSTERS
H,AMBLING,	A,MORTISE	B,ITCHER	B,OOZIEST
R,AMBLING	A,MOUNTED	D,ITCHING	B,ORDURES
H,ARBOURS	A,NEARING	H,ITCHING	B,RACKETS
M,ARRIAGE	A,PIARIST	P,ITCHING	B,RAIDING
T,ARROWED	A,PLASTIC	B,LACKING	B,RAILING
P,ARTICLE	A,POSTILS	C,LACKING	T,RAILING
ATROPIN,E	A,READING	S,LACKING	B,RAINING
ATOMISE,R	A,SCENDED	B,LADDERS	D,RAINING
AUDITOR,Y	A,SCRIBED	B,LADDERY	G,RAINING
AUTOMAT,A	A,SHAMING	B,LANKIER	T,RAINING
L,AUREATE	A,SLAKING	B,LASTERS	B,RAISING
H,AUTEURS	A,SPIRING	P,LASTERS	F,RAISING
T,AUTONYM	A,SPORTED	B,LASTING	P,RAISING
L,AWFULLY	A,STEROID	B,LATHERS	B,RANCHED
L,AWNIEST	A,STOUNDS	B,LAUDING	B,RANCHER
T,AWNIEST	A,VAILING	B,LEACHED	B,RANDIES
Y,AWNIEST	A,VERSION	B,LEAKIER	B,RANKING
D,AWNINGS	A,VERTING	B,LEARING	C,RANKING
F,AWNINGS	A,VIATORS	C,LEARING	P,RANKING
Y,AWNINGS	A,VOIDERS	B,LENDING	B,RATLING
F,ALTERED	A,VOUCHED	B,LETTING	B,RATCHET

B,RATTISH	BURNOUS,E	C,LACKING	C,RASHING
B,RATTLED	C,ANTINGS	C,LACKERS	C,RATCHES
P,RATTLED	P,ANTINGS	C,LAMMING	C,REAMIER
B,RATTLES	W,ANTINGS	C,LAMPING	C,REAMING
P,RATTLED	CANZONE,T	C,LATCHED	C,REEKIER
B,REACHED	CAPELIN,E	C,LEANING	C,RESTING
P,REACHED	CAPITAN,O	C,LEARING	C,RICKING
B,REACHES	CARACOL,E	C,LEAVING	C,RICKETS
P,REACHES	CARABIN,E	C,LEMMING	C,RINGING
B,REAMING	O,CARINAS	C,LICKERS	C,RINGERS
C,REAMING	C,AROUSED	C,LICKING	C,RISPING
D,REAMING	C,AROUSAL	C,LIMBERS	C,ROCHETS
B,REASTED	C,AROUSER	C,LIMBING	C,ROCKERY
B,REECHED	CENTAUR,Y	C,LINGIER	C,ROCKING
B,REECHES	C,ENTERED	C,LINKING	C,ROCKETS
B,REEDERS	T,ENTERED	C,LIPPING	C,ROOKING
B,REEDING	C,HAIRING	C,LITTERS	C,ROTCHES
B,RICKING	C,HAINING	C,LOCKERS	C,ROUPIER
P,RICKING	C,HAUNTER	C,LOCKING	C,ROUPING
T,RICKING	C,HARKING	C,LOPPING	C,ROWDIES
B,RICKLES	S,HARKING	C,LOSINGS	C,RUDDLED
P,RICKLES	C,HAPPING	C,LOTTING	C,RUMBLED
B,RIDGING	W,HAPPING	C,LOURING	C,RUMBLES
F,RIDGING	C,HARMFUL	C,LOUTING	C,RUMMIER
B,RIGHTLY	C,HATTING	C,LOWNING	C,RUMMIES
B,RIGHTEN	.C,HATTERS	C,LUMBERS	C,RUMPLED
F,RIGHTEN	S,HATTERS	C,LUMPIER	C,RUMPLES
B,RINGERS	C,HEATERS	C,LUNCHES	DEBOUCH,E
B,RINGING	C,HEATING	C,LUSTERS	DECLASS,E
B,RISKING	C,HIDINGS	COMPLIN,E	DECUPLE,D
F,RISKING	C,HILLIER	COURANT,E	DECUPLE,S
B,ROACHED	C,HILLING	C,OVERING	D,ELATION
B,ROCKETS	S,HILLING	C,OVERTLY	D,ELUSION
C,ROCKETS	C,HIPPING	C,RACKERS	D,ELUSIVE
B,ROILING	S,HIPPING	C,RACKING	D,ELUSORY
B,ROOKING	C,HOUSING	C,RAFTING	DEMENTI,A
C,ROOKING	C,HUCKLES	C,RAGGIER	D,EMERSED
B,ROOMIER	C,HUFFIER	C,RAMMERS	D,EMERGED
B,ROOMING	C,HUMMING	C,RAMMING	D,EMERGES
BROWNIE,R	C,HUNKIER	C,RAMPING	D,EMITTED
G,ROOMING	C,HUNTERS	C,RANKING	D,EMOTION
B,RUSHIER	C,INCHING	C,RANKLED	D,ENOUNCE
B,RUSHING	CINEAST,E	C,RANKLES	D,EPILATE
C,RUSHING	CINEREA,L	C,RAPPING	D,EPURATE

D,ESCRIBE	S,EATINGS	R,ENOUNCE	F,LAMMING
D,EVOLVED	EBRIATE,D	N,EOLITHS	F,LAPPING
D,EVOLVES	E,CAUDATE	L,EPIDOTE	F,LASHING
D,HURRIES	E,CLOSING	E,RADIATE	F,LAWLESS
DISJOIN,T	E,COSTATE	E,RASURES	F,LECTION
D,RABBLED	NH,EDGINGS	E,RECTION	F,LEDGIER
D,RABBLES	W,EDGINGS	E,RECTORS	F,LEERING
D,RABBLER	E,DENTATE	E,RODENTS	F,LICKERS
D,RAFFISH	H,EDGIEST	E,SCALADE	F,LICKING
D,RAFTERS	L,EDGIEST	E,SCALADO	F,LIGHTED
D,RAILING	S,EDGIEST	E,SCAPING	F,LIMPING
D,RAINING	S,EDITION	E,SCARPED	F,LITTERS
D,READERS	B,EERIEST	E,SPECIAL	G,LITTERS
D,REAMERS	L,EERIEST	E,SPOUSAL	F,LOPPING
D,REAMIER	P,EERIEST	E,SQUIRES	F,LOUNDER
D,REAMING	L,EGALITY	E,STATING	F,LOURIER
D,RIFTING	R,EGALITY	E,STOPPED	F,LOUTING
D,RILLING	L,EGGIEST	E,STRANGE	F,LOWERED
D,RIPPING	R,EJECTOR	E,STRAYED	F,LUMPING
D,ROILING	E,LANCING	F,ETCHING	F,LUSHING
D,ROOPING	E,LAPSING	L,ETCHING	F,LUTINGS
D,ROOKING	G,ELASTIC	R,ETCHING	F,RAGMENT
DUODENA,L	D,ELATION	M,ETHANES	B,RAISING
D,WELLING	G,ELATION	F,ETTLING	F,RAISING
D,WINDLES	R,ELATION	P,ETTLING	P,RAISING
B,EARINGS	D,ELATING	S,ETTLING	C,RANKING
G,EARINGS	R,ELATING	H,EURAKAS	F,RANKING
H,EARINGS	R,ELATERS	E,VALUATE	C,RAPPING
S,EARINGS	G,ELDINGS	E,VERTING	F,RAPPING
T,EARINGS	E,LECTION	E,VERSION	T,RAPPING
W,EARINGS	E,LECTORS	R,EVERTED	F,RETTING
G,EARLESS	E,LEGISTS	L,EVIRATE	B,RIDGING
T,EARLESS	E,LEVATOR	E,VOLUTES	F,RIDGING
Y,EARDING	S,ELFHOOD	E,VOLVING	B,RIGHTEN
L,EARNING	E,MERSION	E,VULGATE	F,RIGHTEN
Y,EARNING	E,MISSION	F,ACTIONS	D,RILLING
L,EARNERS	E,MISSIVE	P,ACTIONS	F,RILLING
W,EANLING	E,MOTIONS	F,ADDLING	F,RISKERS
Y,EANLING	E,NATIONS	F,AERIEST	F,RISKFUL
F,EASTING	B,ENDINGS	FEDAYEE,N	F,RISKIER
R,EASTING	L,ENDINGS	FOOTLES,S	F,RISKING
Y,EASTING	M,ENDINGS	F,ITCHIER	F,RITTING
B,EATINGS	S,ENDINGS	F,LAKIEST	F,RITTERS
H,EATINGS	R,ENEWING	FLAMING,O	F,ROCKING

F,ROUNCES	G,REAVING	INTERNE,E	E,MIGRATE
C,RUMPLED	G,REINING	ISOCHOR,E	E,MIGRANT
F,RUMPLED	G,RIDDLES	H,ITCHIER	MORCEAU,X
C,RUMPLES	D,RILLING	J,AUNTIES	S,MOTHERY
F,RUMPLES	G,RILLING	J,OUSTING	M,UNITION
FUSAROL,E	G,RIMIEST	K,NIGHTLY	MUSICAL,E
F,UTILITY	G,RINNING	K,NIGHTED	NARGILE,H
GALOPIN,G	G,RITTING	LACINIA,E	NOCTURN,E
GELATIN,E	B,ROOMING	LACUNAR,Y	NORTHER,N
GENERAL,E	G,ROOMING	LAMBAST,E	N,OVATION
G,HARRIES	G,ROUPING	LAMINAR,Y	OCTUPLE,T
GIRASOL,E	G,ROUSING	LANOLIN,E	ORDINAR,Y
G,LAIRIER	G,ROUTING	LARGESS,E	OUTRIDE,R
C,LEANING	G,RUBBERS	LARVATE,D	OUTDOOR,S
G,LEANING	G,UTTERED	L,AZURITE	OUTGROW,N
G,LEAMING	S,HAMBLED	L,ETCHING	R,OUTINGS
G,LIMMERS	S,HAMBLES	F,ETCHING	OUTROPE,R
G,LISTENS	W,HAPPING	R,ETCHING	OVERLIE,R
G,LISTERS	HARMOST,Y	LICENSE,D	C,OVERING
G,LITTERS	S,HARPERS	LICENSE,E	D,OVERING
G,LOAMING	T,HATCHED	LICENSE,R	OVERLIE,R
B,LOOMING	T,HATCHER	B,LIGHTED	OVERSEA,S
G,LOOMING	S,HATTERS	F,LIGHTED	OVERSEE,N
F,LOUTING	S,HEALING	P,LIGHTED	OVERSEE,R
G,LOUTING	W,HELMING	S,LIGHTED	OVERSEW,N
F,LOWERED	W,HELPING	B,LIGHTER	OVERSOW,N
G,LOWERED	S,HERRIES	P,LIGHTER	OXIDISE,R
G,LUMPIER	W,HERRIES	S,LIGHTER	OZONISE,R
G,LUMPISH	HETAIRA,I	LINGULA,R	OZONIZE,R
G,OFFERED	W,HINGING	LOCUSTA,E	PANICLE,D
GONIDIA,L	W,HINNIES	L,OMENTUM	PANTILE,D
D,RABBLED	W,HISTING	LUPULIN,E	PAPILLA,E
G,RABBLED	W,HITHERS	MADRASA,H	PAPILLA,R
D,RABBLES	H,OARIEST	MANDRIL,L	PATELLA,E
G,RABBLES	S,HOCKING	MANDIOC,A	PATELLA,R
G,RAFTERS	HOLESOM,E	MARQUIS,E	PEARLIN,G
C,RAFTING	W,HOOPERS	MATADOR,E	PEARLIN,S
G,RAFTING	H,OTTERED	MATELOT,E	PEDICLE,D
B,RAINIER	S,HUNTING	MATRICE,S	PEEKABO,O
G,RAINIER	IDOLISE,R	MAUVEIN,E	P,EERIEST
B,RAINING	C,INCHING	MAXILLA,E	PERFECT,I
D,RAINING	P,INCHING	MEDULLA,E	PERIDOT,E
G,RAINING	W,INCHING	EMICATE,D	PERSICO,T
G,RASPING	INCISOR,Y	EMICATE,S	PERSONA,L

P,ETTLING	P,REFACES	RAMPIRE,D	S,CHILLER
PISTOLE,T	P,REFORMS	RANCHER,O	S,COFFING
P,ITCHIER	P,REGNANT	RAPHIDE,S	S,COOPERS
PLANULA,R	P,RELATES	R,APHIDES	S,COOPING
P,LASHING	P,REMISED	RATTLIN,E	S,CORNERS
P,LEACHED	P,REMISES	RATTLIN,G	S,CORNING
P,LEADERS	P,REMORSE	REGIMEN,T	S,COUPING
P,LEADING	P,REMOVED	REGRATE,R	S,COWPING
P,LEASERS	P,REMOVES	REHEARS,E	S,COUTERS
P,LEASING	P,RESCIND	RENEGUE,R	S,COWLING
P,LIGHTED	P,RESENTS	RENEGUE,D	S,COWRIES
P,LOTTING	P,RESERVE	RENEGUE,S	S,CRABBED
P,LUCKIER	P,RESIDED	RESIDUA,L	S,CRAGGED
P,LUMBAGO	P,RESIDES	RICKSHA,W	S,CRAMMED
P,LUMPERS	P,RESUMED	R,OARIEST	S,CRAPING
P,LUMPIER	P,RESUMES	RONDEAU,X	S,CRAPPED
P,LUMPING	P,REVIEWS	ROUNDLE,T	S,CRATING
PLUMULA,E	P,RICKERS	RUBELLA,N	S,CRAWLER
PLUMULA,R	P,RICKING	SABURRA,L	S,CRAWLED
P,LUNGING	P,RICKLED	SACRIST,Y	S,CREAKED
P,LUSHIER	P,RICKLES	SAGITTA,L	S,CREWING
PODAGRA,L	P,RIMMING	S,ALLOWED	S,CRIBBLE
POLITIC,O	P,RINKING	S,ALLYING	S,CRIMPED
PONCEAU,X	PRONOTA,L	SARMENT,A	S,CUDDLED
PORTIER,E	P,ROOFING	SAVANNA,H	S,CUDDLES
P,OTTERED	P,ROSIEST	E,SCALADE	S,CUFFING
P,OUTINGS	PROTEGE,E	E,SCALADO	S,CULLING
PRACTIC,E	P,UNITION	S,CAMPERS	S,CULLERS
P,RAISING	P,UNITIVE	S,CAMPING	S,CULLION
P,RANCING	PTERYLA,E	S,CANNERS	S,CUMBERS
P,RANKING	QUADRAT,E	S,CANNING	S,CUNNERS
P,RANKLED	QUARTER,N	S,CANDENT	S,CUPPERS
P,RANKLES	QUARTET,T	S,CATING	S,CURRIES
P,RATINGS	QUIDDIT,Y	S,CANTIER	S,CURRIED
P,RATTLES	QUIDDLE,R	S,CANTLED	S,CURVIER
P,RATTLED	QUINTET,T	S,CANTLES	S,CUTCHES
P,RATTLER	B,RAISING	SCAPULA,R	S,CUTTLES
P,RATTLES	F,RAISING	S,CARIOUS	S,EDGIEST
P,REACHED	P,RAISING	S,CARPING	S,ELECTED
P,RECEDED	C,RANKING	S,CARTING	S,ELECTOR
P,RECEDES	F,RANKING	S,CATTING	SEPTETT,E
P,REDATED	C,RAPPING	S,CATCHES	SEQUELA,E
P,REDATES	F,RAPPING	S,CATTERY	SERPULA,E
P,REFACED	T,RAPPING	S,CATTIER	SESTETT,E

177

SESTETT,O	S,KITTLED	S,MOUCHED	S,PINIEST
S,ETTLING	S,KITTLES	S,NAILERY	S,PIRATED
SEXTETT,E	S,LACKERS	S,NAPPING	S,PITTING
S,FORZATO	S,LACKING	S,NAPPIER	S,PITCHER
S,HACKLED	A,SLAKING	S,NECKING	S,PLASHED
S,HACKLES	S,LAMMING	S,NEEZING	S,PLATTER
S,HADDOCK	S,LANDERS	S,NIBBING	S,PLAYING
S,HAFTING	S,LAPPING	S,NICKERS	A,SPORTED
S,HALLOWS	S,LASHERS	S,NICKING	S,PONTOON
S,HAMMERS	S,LASHING	S,NIFFIER	S,POOKING
S,HAMMING	SLATTER,N	S,NIFTIER	S,POOLING
S,HAMBLED	SLATTER,Y	S,NIGGERS	S,PORTERS
S,HAMBLES	S,LEAVING	S,NIGGLED	S,PORTIER
S,HANKING	S,LEDGERS	S,NIGGLER	S,POTTING
S,HARKING	S,LICKERS	S,NIGGLES	S,POUTERS
S,HARPERS	S,LICKING	S,NIPPERS	S,POUTING
S,HATTERS	SLIDDER,Y	S,NIPPING	S,PRAYERS
S,HAVINGS	S,LIGHTED	S,NOBBIER	S,PRAYING
S,HEADING	S,LIGHTER	S,NODDLING	S,PRIGGED
S,HEALING	S,LIMIEST	S,NUZZLING	S,PRINTED
S,HEARERS	S,LINKING	SOREDIA,L	S,PRINTER
S,HEARING	S,LIPPIER	S,PALLING	S,PUDDING
S,HELLING	S,LIPPING	S,PANNING	S,PURRING
S,HELVING	S,LITTERS	S,PANGING	S,PUTTERS
S,HERRIES	S,LIVERED	S,PARABLE	S,QUAILED
S,HEUCHES	S,LOOMING	S,PARGING	S,QUASHED
S,HILLING	S,LOPPING	S,PARKING	S,QUIRING
S,HINNIES	S,LOTTING	S,PARKISH	S,QUIRTED
S,HIPPING	S,LUBBERS	S,PARLING	S,TABLING
S,HOCKING	S,LUMBERS	S,PATTING	S,TACKING
S,HOOTERS	S,LUMPIER	S,PAWNERS	S,TALKING
S,HOOTING	S,LUMPING	S,PAWNING	S,TALKERS
S,HOPPERS	S,LUSHIER	S,PEAKING	S,TALLAGE
S,HOPPING	S,LUSHING	S,PECKING	STAMINA,L
S,HUNTERS	S,MALLING	SPECULA,R	STAMPED,E
S,HUNTING	S,MATTERS	S,PEELERS	S,TAMPERS
S,HUTTING	S,MATCHED	S,PEELING	S,TAMPING
SILICON,E	S,MELLING	S,PENDING	S,TARRIER
S,KELTERS	S,MELTING	SPICULA,R	S,TARRING
S,KEPPING	S,MIRKIER	S,PIKELET	S,TARTING
S,KETCHES	S,MOCKING	S,PILLING	S,TARTISH,
S,KILLING,	S,MOOTING	S,PILLAGE	S,TASHING
S,KIPPING	S,MOORING	S,PINNERS	S,TEAMERS
S,KIPPERS	S,MOTHERY	S,PINNING	S,TEAMING

STEARIN,E	S,TUBBIER	T,ALLYING	T,RIMMING
S,TELLING	S,TUMBLED	TAMARIN,D	T,RIPPERS
S,TENDING	S,TUMBLER	TAMBOUR,A	T,RIPPING
S,TENTING	S,TUMBLES	TARTANE,D	T,ROCKING
A,STHENIC	S,TUMPIER	TARTANE,S	T,ROLLERS
S,TICKERS	S,TUMPING	T,ENTERED	T,ROLLING
S,TICKING	S,TUNNING	TESSERA,E	T,ROOPING
STICKLE,D	S,ULLAGES	TESSERA,L	T,ROTTERS
STICKLE,R	S,WADDLED	T,HACKING	T,ROTTING
STICKLE,S	S,WADDLER	T,HATCHED	T,ROUBLES
S,TIDDIES	S,WADDLES	THERIAC,A	T,ROUNCES
S,TILLERS	S,WALIEST	T,HORNING	T,ROUSERS
S,TILLAGE	S,WALLETS	T,HORNIER	T,ROUTERS
S,TILLING	S,WALLOWS	T,HUMPING	T,ROUTING
S,TINGING	S,WAPPING	T,INKLING	T,RUCKING
S,TINKERS	S,WARMERS	TONTINE,R	T,RUCKLED
S,TINKING	S,WARMING	TONTINE,S	T,RUCKLES
S,TINTERS	S,WARTIER	TORMINA,L	T,RUFFLED
S,TINTIER	S,WASHIER	T,OTTERED	T,RUFFLES
S,TINTING	S,WASHING	TRACHEA,E	TRUMEAU,X
S,TIPPLED	S,WATCHES	TRACHEA,L	T,RUMPING
S,TIPPLER	S,WEARERS	T,RAMPING	T,RUMDLED
S,TIPPLES	S,WEARING	T,RANTING	T,RUNDLES
STOMATA,L	S,WEEPIER	T,RAPPERS	T,RUSTIER
S,TOOLING	S,WEEPING	T,RAPPING	T,RUSTING
S,TOPPERS	S,WELLING	T,READERS	T,RUTHFUL
S,TOPPING	S,WELTING	T,READING	S,TUMPIER
S,TOPLESS	S,WELTERS	T,REMBLED	TUTELAR,Y
S,TOTTERS	S,WILLERS	T,REMBLES	T,WADDLED
S,TOWAGES	S,WILLING	T,RENDING	T,WADDLER
S,TOWINGS	S,WINDLES	T,RENTALS	T,WADDLES
S,TRAIKED	S,WINGERS	TRIARCH,Y	T,WANGLED
S,TRAINED	S,WINGING	TRIBUTE,R	T,WANGLES
S,TRAINER	S,WINKING	T,RICKING	T,WATTLED
S,TRAMPED	S,WISHING	B,RICKLES	T,WATTLES
S,TRANGLE	S,WITCHED	P,RICKLES	T,WILLING
S,TRICKLE	S,WITCHES	T,RICKLES	T,WINNING
S,TRIDENT	S,WITHERS	TRICKER,Y	T,WINIEST
S,TRIKING	S,WORDING	TRICORN,E	T,WINGING
S,TRIPPER	SYMBION,T	T,RIFLERS	T,WINKING
S,TRIPPED	SYNOVIA,L	T,RIFLING	T,WINKLED
S,TROLLED	A,SYSTOLE	T,RIGGERS	T,WINKLES
S,TROLLER	TACHISM,E	TRILOBE,D	T,WINTERS
S,TROKING	TACHIST,E	T,RILLING	T,WISTING

T,WITTING	B,UTTERED	W,HOOPING
T,WITCHED	G,UTTERED	W,HOPPERS
T,WITCHES	M,UTTERED	W,HOPPING
UNCLOSE,D	A,VOUCHED	W,OOZIEST
UNCLOSE,S	V,AGILITY	W,OUNDIER
UNHOUSE,D	V,AIRIEST	WRANGLE,D
UNHOUSE,D	VARIOLA,R	WRANGLE,R
UNLOOSE,D	VASCULA,R	WRANGLE,S
UNLOOSE,N	V,AUNTERS	W,RAPPERS
UNLOOSE,S	V,ENATION	W,RAPPING
UNPLACE,E	VERRUCA,E	WREATHE,D
UNPLACE,S	VESTURE,D	WREATHE,N
UNREAVE,D	VESTURE,R	WREATHE,R
UNREAVE,S	VESTURE,S	WREATHE,S
UNREEVE,D	VINTAGE,D	W,RECKING
UNREEVE,S	VINTAGE,R	W,RESTERS
UNSCALE,D	VINTAGE,S	W,RESTING
UNSCALE,S	VITAMIN,E	W,RICKING
UNSHALE,D	VITELLI,N	W,RINGERS
UNSHALE,S	W,ALLOWED	W,RINGING
UNTWINE,D	A,WANTING	XANTHIN,E
UNTWINE,S	W,ANTINGS	Y,AWNINGS
UNVOICE,D	W,ARRAYED	Y,AWNIEST
UNVOICE,S	W,ARTIEST	Y,EANLING
UNWEAVE,D	W,EANLING	Y,EARDING
UNWEAVE,S	W,EARINGS	Y,EARNING
UPRAISE,D	W,EDGINGS	Y,EASTING
UPRAISE,D	W,HACKING	A,ZYMITES
UPSTAGE,D	W,HANGING	
UPSTAGE,S	W,HAPPING	
UPSTARE,D	W,HEELING	
UPSTARE,S	W,HELMING	
UPSURGE,D	W,HELPING	
UPSURGE,S	W,HERRIES	
UREDINE,S	W,HETTING	
URETHAN,E	W,HINGING	
URETHRA,L	W,HINNIES	
URETHRA,S	W,HIPPING	
UTILISE,D	W,HIPPIER	
UTILISE,S	W,HIPSTER	
UTILISE,R	W,HISSING	
UTILIZE,D	W,HISTING	
UTILIZE,R	W,HITHERS	
UTILIZE,S	W,HOOPERS	

Eight-letter words becoming nine-letter words

ALIZARIN,E
AMBROSIA,L
AMBROSIA,N
A,PERIODIC
D,ALLIANCE
R,ANTIPOLE
AQUATINT,A
R,AREFYING
A,SCENDING
A,SEXUALLY
A,SPORTING
A,STOUNDED
A,STRINGED
A,TROPHIED
AVENTAIL,E
BASILICA,L
A,BATEMENT
A,BASEMENT
H,ARBOURED
CANEPHOR,A
CANEPHOR,E
CAPITULA,R
CAPONIER,E
CHAPERON,E
C,HASTENED
C,HASTENER
C,HIDLINGS
(see Chitterling)
C,HILDINGS
C,HOROLOGY
C,LAVATION
C,LEAVINGS
C,LITTERED
C,LINGIEST
S,CRAWLER
CREEPIES,T
S,CRIMPIER
S,CRUMMIER
S,CRUMPIER
DEDICATE,E
DIRECTOR,Y
DISCOVER,T
DISCOVER,Y
DISGRACE,R

DISTRAIN,T
P,EARLIEST
B,EERINESS
W,EDGEWISE
D,EDUCTION
R,EDUCTION
S,EDUCTION
D,EJECTION
R,EMIGRATE
R,EMISSION
C,ENTERING
T,ENTERING
R,EMISSIVE
D,EMITTING
R,EMITTING
EMPHASIS,E
P,ETIOLATE
F,LITTERED
G,LITTERED
HALFTIME,R
S,HALLOWED
HARMALIN,E
S,HEATHIER
W,HITHERED
W,HOLESOME
HOROLOGE,R
S,HOVELLED
HUCKSTER,Y
F,ITCHIEST
H,ITCHIEST
P,ITCHIEST
F,LAUGHTER
S,LAUGHTER
L,IMITABLE
E,LOCUTION
B,LOUSIEST
MAGNESIA,N
MAINLINE,D
MAINLINE,R
MAINLINE,S
MALINGER,Y
MANDATOR,Y
MANDOLIN,E
MANIFEST,O

MANUBRIA,L
MARGARIN,E
S,MATTERED
MEDIATOR,Y
MEDICINE,R
MUSCADIN,E
MURICATE,D
NEBULISE,R
H,ODOMETER,
W,OUNDIEST
OVERFLOW,N
OVERLADE,N
OVERTIME,R
PANTABLE,S
PARTITUR,A
PASTORAL,E
PENDICLE,R
PENTARCH,Y
S,PECULATE
PENTOSAN,E
O,PINIONED
E,PISTOLET
S,PLASHIER
S,PORTABLE
PRODITOR,Y
PRODROMI,C
PROVEDOR,E
PULSATOR,Y
E,RADICATE
C,RAFTSMAN
C,RANKLING
RATIONAL,E
B,RATTLING
P,RATTLING
G,RAVELLED
T,RAVELLED
B,REACHING
P,REACHING
C,REAMIEST
D,REAMIEST
P,RELATION
T,REMBLING
P,REMOTION
P,REMOVING

P,RESENTER	C,RUSTIEST	A,TROPHIED
P,RESIDENT	T,RUSTIEST	S,TROUTING
P,RESIDING	T,RUTHLESS	T,URGENTLY
RETINUNA,E	SPELDRIN,G	B,UTTERING
RETINULA,R	A,SPIRATED	G,UTTERING
P,REVIEWED	SPRINGAL,D	M,UTTERING
P,REVISION	A,STRINGED	VERATRIN,E
RICERCAR,E	SLUGHORN,E	VERTEBRA,E
P,RICKLIER	SYNEDRIA,L	VERTEBRA,L
T,RICKLIER	TRACHEID,E	VIGILANT,E
P,ROOFLESS	S,TRAMPING	VOCALISE,R
C,ROUPIEST	TRAPEZIA,L	SAMINDAR,I
S,TRIPLING	SEMINDAR,Y	ZEMINDAR,I

N.B. A few plural nouns like PRETTIES will take a T at the end to make
a superlative and some superlatives like RUSTIEST will take letters
before them, e.g. C or T.

SEATING plus other letters

A = SAGINATE
B = BEATINGS
D = SEDATING STEADING
E = SAGENITE
F = FEASTING
H = HEATINGS
L = GELATINS STEALING
M = MANGIEST STEAMING TEAMINGS MINTAGES
R = GANISTER INGRATES REASTING GANTRIES
S = SEATINGS TEASINGS
T = ESTATING
V = VINTAGES
W = SWEATING

ANAGRAM ANSWERS

1. GRANITE/INGRATE
2. RESPECT/SPECTRE
3. REWARDS/WARDERS
4. DEARING/GRADINE/GRAINED
5. CLAIMED/DECIMAL/DECLAIM
6. ALAMORT
7. AMARINE
8. REPENTS/SERPENT
9. ALIENOR/ALERION
10. ALATION
11. FILIATE
12. NIGRINE
13. FOUNDER/REFOUND
14. COTERIE
15. DIVERGE/GRIEVED
16. GUERDON/UNDERGO
17. TINGLER/TRINGLE
18. URANITE/TAURINE/URINATE
19. POINTER/PTERION/TROPINE
20. LURDANE/RUNDALE
21. TRIGONE
22. GENTIER/TEARING/TREEING
23. IGNITER/TIGRINE

24. RINGENT
25. ENTRAIL/RATLINE/RELIANT/RETINAL/TRENAIL
26. ITERANT/NITRATE/TARTINE/TERTIAN
27. TERCINE/ENTICER
28. CRINATE/CITREAN/NACRITE
29. CITRINE/CRINITE/NERITIC
30. HENOTIC
31. NOMINAL
32. CHAGRIN/CHARING
33. ETAERIO
34. MISDONE
35. NOTITIA
36. GROINED/NEGROID/REDOING
37. FLANEUR
38. CHEERLY
39. THEREAT
40. RESPELT/SPELTER
41. PALTERS/PLATERS/PSALTER/STAPLER
42. ASTERIA/ATRESIA
43. RETINOL
44. ETHERIC
45. INFARCT/INFRACT
46. CANTRIP
47. DOLERIN
48. EATINGS/INGESTA/SIGNATE/TANGIES/TEASING/
   . TSIGANE
49. ROSIEST/SORTIES
50. DELAINE
51. ETHERIN/THEREIN
52. COSTERS/ESCORTS/SECTORS/SCOTERS
53. RECUSED/REDUCES/RESCUED/SEDUCER
54. DOPIEST/PODITES/POSITED/SOPITED/TOPSIDE
55. GESTAPO/POTAGES
56. TEACUPS
57. ARSHINE
58. DEWITTS
59. DESPOIL/DIPLOES/DIPOLES/SOLIPED
60. DIAPERS/DESPAIR/ASPIRED
61. NOTABLE